Human Trafficking Amidst Interlocking Systems of Exploitation

A Focus on Pakistan

Human Trafficking Amidst Interlocking Systems of Exploitation

A Focus on Pakistan

Farhan Navid Yousaf & Bandana Purkayastha

frontpage

frontpage
www.frontpagepublications.com

First published 2015

Frontpage Publications Limited
Level 2, 13 John Prince's Street, London W1G 0JR, United Kingdom

Frontpage
Level B, 76 B B Ganguly Street, Kolkata 700012, India

British Library Cataloguing in Publishing Data
A catalogue record for this book is available from the British Library

ISBN: 978 93 81043 15 8

Printed in India
By Sadhana Udyog
76 B B Ganguly Street, Kolkata 700012, India

Typeset by Compuset International
85 Park Street, Kolkata 700016, India

Contents

Acknowledgements

Conducting research on human trafficking, especially which involves interviewing trafficked persons, is indeed a challenging task. This study would not have been possible without support and encouragement of many individuals and organisations. We are particularly indebted to Shameela Ahmed, Muhammad Suleman and Naveed-ul-Haq for their continuous support in collecting data for this study in Pakistan. We would like to thank the Human Rights Institute at the University of Connecticut, USA for awarding the Graduate Student Human Rights Research Grant that enabled Farhan Navid Yousaf to travel to Pakistan to collect data. Finally, we would like to thank all the participants of this study for their time and sharing their experiences and views.

Abbreviations

FIA	Federal Investigation Agency
IOM	International Organization for Migration
NGO	Non-governmental Organisation
P&CHTO	Prevention & Control of Human Trafficking Ordinance
SAARC	South Asian Association for Regional Cooperation
TIP Report	United States Department of State Trafficking in Persons Report
TVPA	Trafficking Victims Protection Act
UN	United Nations
UNESCO	United Nations Educational, Scientific and Cultural Organization
UNHCHR	United Nations High Commissioner for Human Rights
UNHCR	United Nations High Commissioner for Refugees
UNODC	United Nations Office on Drugs and Crime

Introduction

> In May 2014, *Newsweek*, the American weekly news magazine, reported a story about Somaly Mam, a Cambodian woman, who had become known around the world, especially among people who worked on anti-trafficking initiatives, as a relentless crusader for rescuing women and girls trapped as sex-slaves. Discussing this story, Grant (2014) pointed out that the emphasis on those who are trafficked for sex—and the rescue missions to save them—overshadow other forms of trafficking which affect many more people every day. Grant's Op-Ed, in *The New York Times*, ends with strong words of warning. She argued that ending sex trafficking will require going beyond the current 'industry' that is set up to fight sex trafficking; it requires us to move beyond sex trafficking and consider the larger question of human trafficking and the factors which make it difficult to combat.

Trafficking in human beings is neither new nor invisible. From the late 20th century, especially, concerted activism by non-governmental organisations (NGOs) and an unprecedented level of efforts initiated through national laws in different parts of the world and international human rights conventions have made more people aware of the ambit of human trafficking. In 2002, Mary Robinson, who was the United Nations High Commissioner for Human Rights (UNHCHR), released the UN Recommended Principles and Guidelines on Human Rights and Human Trafficking (http://www.ohchr.org/Documents/Publications/Traffickingen.pdf). This document offers clear and practical human rights-based guidelines to *prevent* trafficking and to *protect* the rights of trafficked persons. Yet, even as many policies have been passed in different countries, billions of dollars have been spent, and many efforts to combat trafficking are underway, we have not been able to eradicate the practices that degrade human beings to the level of commodities. Trafficking continues to remain a fundamental moral challenge to all those who believe in the principles of humanity and human rights.

Why is human trafficking so widespread? A range of countries, rich and poor, are now on record as being receivers and senders of humans-as-traffic. Human trafficking also appears to have grown rapidly in the last few decades. The United Nations estimates human trafficking as the second largest, and the fastest growing criminal industry in the world.[1] Although we do not, as yet, have consistently reliable and valid statistics on human trafficking, drawing on a variety of studies, scholars and practitioners estimate that millions of people are trafficked all over the world annually. Are these greater numbers a reflection of better reporting? In other words, is the increase in human trafficking simply a reflection of accurate data? Or has the scope—and consequently the markets for trafficked humans—grown over the last few decades?

We attempt to answer some of these questions in this discourse. We draw upon gender and human rights perspectives to analyse trafficking. One of our primary objectives is to present some of the factors that enhance vulnerability of women and men to trafficking. We examine the issue of trafficking at both micro and macro levels. We look into some of the victims' experiences to identify factors that make them vulnerable to trafficking. We also analyse the disjuncture between international, regional and local policies and guidelines. A critical aspect of this understanding relates to how trafficking is defined. We expand the notion of trafficking from sex trafficking to human trafficking as a profit-making enterprise with human beings as the commodity for sale or exchange. We go beyond sex trafficking—which is the subject of most of the gender scholarship—and International Labour Organization's (ILO) emphasis on labour trafficking to include trafficking in organs. Trafficking is about exploiting human beings while draining them of humanity, so we pay attention to the marketability of parts of human bodies, including organs as these fall within the web of exploitation.

Examining the experiences of trafficked persons, we argue that trafficking occurs within the context of interlocking systems of class/gender/race/ethnic/age structural inequalities. We also emphasise that trafficking occurs within a continuum of violence, ranging from public violence such as wars and intra-state conflict, to private, home-based gendered violence. Threats and/or experience of these diverse types of violence enhance the vulnerabilities associated with entrenched structural inequalities. As a result, some segments of society remain exposed to exploitation, often repeatedly, by traffickers. Thus, we argue, *trafficking might occur repeatedly within a person's life course, though not for the same purpose, and not in the same way*. A person may be trafficked for sexual exploitation at one stage in her/his life and then end up as bonded labour. At the same time, we show that the general failure to understand the entire spectrum of underlying structures that lead to trafficking have channelled efforts to address trafficking in limited ways. Thus, despite the tapestry of international statements and conventions, at the ground level, policies often remain inadequate to address the root causes of trafficking. Nor are many initiatives designed to protect and support victims for a longer term; often there are few resources to ensure their long-term human security.

Our related objective is to discuss the problem of inadequate data on trafficking. We show that a main impediment to analysing the extent and magnitude of trafficking across the world is the lack of consensus on the definition of trafficking. As a result, different countries and organisations provide varied statistics about trafficking based on their particular assumptions.

Although men, women, boys and girls are trafficked all over the world, both within and across countries, the dominant focus of the literature on trafficking as well as counter-trafficking interventions continue to centre on a subset of trafficking: sex trafficking. Consequently, we know less about trafficking for other purposes—e.g., domestic servitude, bonded labour, organ trade—or how well do the policies and institutions designed to address 'trafficking' reflect an accurate understanding of the multidimensionality of the problem and cumulative vulnerabilities that victims often experience.

Although we draw on the literature on trafficking and comparative data from different countries, this critique primarily focuses on Pakistan. According to the United States Department of State Trafficking in Persons Report (TIP Report hereafter), 2013, Pakistan is a source, transit, and destination country in terms of international trafficking in women, men, and children. A large proportion of trafficking, however, occurs within the country. The TIP Report places Pakistan under the Tier 2 as the Government of Pakistan reportedly does not fully comply with the minimum standards for the elimination of human trafficking; however, it is making significant efforts to do so. We analyse the intersection of economic and political forces that shape trafficking—including the experiences of the victims—in Pakistan. This focus also allows us to emphasise some of the larger global and regional structures that enhance vulnerability of people to trafficking, an aspect that is not often discussed consistently in the literature or policies.

Focusing on the province of Punjab in Pakistan,[2] we use three types of data. At the micro level, we draw upon the life experiences of twenty-five trafficked persons, including fifteen women and ten men. To protect their confidentiality, we use pseudo names, and obfuscate identifying information as we present victims' narratives later in this discourse. In addition, we examine interviews conducted with the stakeholders, including representatives of concerned government departments, international organisations and NGOs working on the issue of human trafficking. Interviews with the stakeholders helped us to study their understanding of trafficking and efficacy of the policy solutions being used. We also analysed trafficking-related legislation and policies to understand who—under what circumstances—qualifies as a victim of trafficking, and how these policies address the needs of trafficked persons.

While there are several studies and debates about trafficking, we expect this study to be useful to scholars and policy makers who wish to go beyond the widely used definitions, and for those who wish to lobby for or design and strengthen more effective anti-trafficking initiatives.

This book is divided into six chapters. **Chapter one** presents background and an overview of human trafficking as a transnational issue. In this chapter, we briefly discuss the evolution of the concept of human trafficking, and factors that enhance vulnerability of people to trafficking. Moreover, we explain reasons that make assessment of magnitude of trafficking difficult, especially with reference to often confusing relationship between trafficking and smuggling.

Chapter two provides a glimpse into trafficking in South Asia and then focuses on the situation in Pakistan. In this chapter, we explain the prevalence and nature of the problem in Pakistan with reference to the contributing factors discussed in chapter one. Focusing on Pakistan, we also analyse how political and economic instability, which is hardly discussed in literature on trafficking, enhances the vulnerability of people to trafficking.

Chapter three examines the issue of human trafficking from a gender perspective, and challenges the gendered assumptions about trafficking through a brief description of feminist debates on sex trafficking and their limitations. We begin by explaining the notion of gendered exploitation as it has been developed by feminist scholars. We show that trafficking is gendered, because men and women of different ages and classes are victimised in different ways. We present some experiences of men and women victims of trafficking to showcase the intersecting gender/class/age factors that made them vulnerable to trafficking. We conclude the chapter by highlighting how the dominant literature on trafficking fails to encapsulate vulnerabilities of men to trafficking.

Chapter four situates the phenomenon of human trafficking within the human rights paradigm. We begin by providing a brief explanation of human rights. People lacking human rights are the most susceptible to trafficking and other forms of exploitation. The experiences of victims show that trafficking constitutes an assault on human dignity and reflects a fundamental violation of their political-economic-social-cultural rights. We then examine the anti-trafficking interventions in Pakistan to emphasise analysing human trafficking through human rights framework.

Chapter five returns to conceptualisation of human trafficking, and examines the gap between definitions, academic literature and practice. In this chapter, we discuss diverse definitions of human trafficking, and analyse how the lack of consensus on defining trafficking influences the eligibility to be considered as a victim of trafficking. Focusing on trafficking legislation and institutional support available to trafficked persons in Pakistan, we demonstrate that narrow understanding of trafficking leads to outcomes that are inadequate to address the root causes of trafficking.

In **chapter six**, while concluding with some reflections on trafficking, we return to some of the discussions we began in chapter one. We reiterate trafficking is a transnational phenomenon that cannot be addressed without international efforts, but these efforts need to go well beyond the rescue models that are most prevalent today. We emphasise the need to use a current definition of gender, i.e. the intersections of gender/class/age and other stratifications to understand the causes and consequences of trafficking. We re-present trafficking as an outcome of power relations emanating from the intersections of local and global structures of inequality, structured through large scale and local violence, supported by societal inaction or misdirected short-term solutions, in need of urgent solutions that actually address the realities of the victims experienced trafficking.

CHAPTER 1
Human Trafficking: An Overview

Our reformers have suddenly made a great discovery: the white slave traffic. The papers are full of these "unheard of conditions" in our midst, and the lawmakers are already planning a new set of laws to check the horror.

How is it that an institution, known to almost every child, should have been discovered so suddenly? How is it that this evil, known to all sociologists, should now be made such an important issue?

It is significant that whenever the public mind is diverted from a great social wrong, a crusade is inaugurated against indecency, gambling, saloons, etc. And what is the result of such crusades? Gambling is increasing, saloons are doing a lively business through back entrances, prostitution is at its height, and the system of pimps and cadets is but aggravated.

To assume that the recent investigation of the white slave traffic by George Kibbe Turner and others (and by the way, a very superficial investigation), has discovered anything new is, to say the least, very foolish. Prostitution was, and is a widespread evil, yet mankind goes on its business, perfectly indifferent to the sufferings and distress of the victims of prostitution. As indifferent, indeed, as mankind has so far remained to our industrial system, of to economic prostitution.

> Only when human sorrows are turned into a toy with glaring colours will baby people become interested, —for a while at least. The people are a very fickle baby that must have new toys every day. The 'righteous' cry against the white slave traffic is such a toy. It serves to amuse the people for a little while, and it will help to create a few more fat political jobs—parasites who stalk about the world as inspectors, investigators, detectives, etc.
>
> What really is the cause of the trade in women? Not merely white women, but yellow and black women as well. Exploitation, of course: the merciless Moloch of capitalism that fattens on underpaid labour, thus driving thousands of women and girls into prostitution. With Mrs. Warren these girls feel, "Why waste your life working for a few shillings a week in a scullery, eighteen hours a day?"
>
> Naturally our reformers say nothing about this cause. They know it well enough, but it doesn't pay to say anything about it. It is much more profitable to play the Pharisee, to pretend an outraged morality, than to go to the bottom of things.
>
> Goldman (1910:2)

We have now begun to consider human trafficking as modern-day slavery and a transnational phenomenon that affects the whole world (Raymond 2002; Ebbe 2008; Birkenthal 2011; Haerens 2012; Wilson 2012), yet the introductory quotation from the turn of the 20th century USA shows that trafficking is not a new phenomenon. According to the estimates of the United Nations, human trafficking has become the second largest criminal industry in the world after drugs, victimising millions of people annually.[3] Shelley (2010) argues that human beings have an added advantage for traffickers over drugs as they can be sold or exploited repeatedly. Consequently, as the UNESCO data show in Figure 1, trafficking in human beings has become one of the most profitable activities, generating more than $31 billion annually (Batstone 2007; Jones 2010; Birkenthal 2011; Kara 2011; Mills 2011).

In this chapter, we provide an overview of trafficking, especially its relationship to slavery and sexual exploitation. Following this, we discuss contemporary understanding of trafficking. We end with a brief discussion on the links between human trafficking and human smuggling.

TRAFFICKING IN A HISTORICAL PERSPECTIVE

According to many scholars (e.g., Bales 2000; Obokata 2006; Othman 2006; Schauer and Wheaton 2006; Aronowitz 2009; Birkenthal 2011), trafficking in human beings is a form of slavery and forced servitude. While all forms of slavery degrade human beings, the specific forms of exploitation and

Figure 1: Value of Trafficking Industry

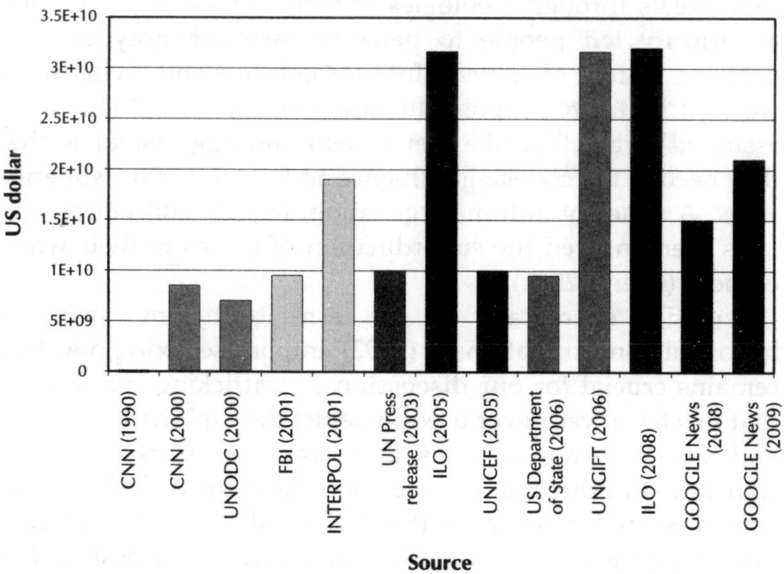

Graph Source: United Nations Educational, Scientific and Cultural Organization (UNESCO)*Trafficking and HIV/AIDS Project*

organisation of human trafficking continue to change over time, staying one step ahead of laws that are created to eradicate these evils. Trafficking survives because trafficking in human beings remains a high-profit global enterprise (Jordan 2002; Schauer and Wheaton 2006; Aronowitz 2009).

While providing a brief history of transition from older to modern forms of slavery and trafficking in human beings, Obokata (2006) notes that though the traces of old forms of slavery can be found in the ancient civilisations of the Middle East and Mediterranean, the practices became more prominent and widespread during the period of the Roman Empire, and subsequently further expanded in different parts of Europe and North America. During the period of Roman Empire, slaves were treated as private property of owners and were frequently used for domestic servitude, partners in sex, and as labourers for the production of local crafts. However, as the African slave trade became more widespread, the concerted effort to justify the exploitation of darker individuals through ideologies of black inferiority and white superiority led people to perceive race (phenotype) as a defining feature of slavery. Inferior cultures and civilisations were attributed to people with dark phenotypes and they were assumed to be child-like (yet violent and aggressive) so that they needed the civilising influence and control of the superior races. A series of anti-miscegenation, labour, and citizenship laws then ensured the subordination of slaves to their white owners (Glenn 2002).

Focusing specifically on the term 'trafficking' within a historical context, Pattanaik (2002) emphasises one point that remains crucial for our discussion of trafficking. She argues that this term was never used to depict the exploitation of men and women from colonies as forced labourers and their transport to other colonies. In fact, the term trafficking was coined with reference to the "white slave trade", mainly describing the white Caucasian women who were assumed to be enslaved through the use of force and deception, and then transported to the colonies as prostitutes to offer sexual services to white male officers. Thus, Pattanaik indicates the racial hierarchies inherent in the use of the term trafficking. On the one hand, trafficking indicated a trade in human beings for prostitution—a gendered form of exploitation. On the other hand, the term was reserved for *white women* who were trafficked for sexual exploitation by white men; the sexual exploitation of non-white women, under conditions of slavery, remained unmarked.

In a similar issue, Obokata (2006) notes that the prohibition of slavery in the United States exemplifies how race was strongly perceived as a defining element of slavery. Slavery was abolished in the United States through the 13th Amendment to the Constitution adopted in December 1865. While interpreting the 13th Amendment in Civil Rights Cases, the Supreme Court differentiated between Roman slavery and American slavery stating that Roman slavery was about enslaving whites, whereas American slavery related only to black Africans.

According to Outshoorn (2005), trafficking and prostitution were linked at the end of the 19th century when rapid socioeconomic changes, mainly caused by industrialisation, urbanisation and unequal distribution of wealth, led to increase in out-migration from Europe. The recruitment and transportation of white women for sex trafficking in 1880s resulted in increased concerns about the free movement of women. At the same time, abolition of prostitution became a main demand of feminism. As a result, since 1904 when trafficking in women was outlawed, international efforts to counter trafficking have continued to move along the same broad trajectory, mainly focused on addressing prostitution while other aspects of trafficking remained less visible. And, as Grant (2014) pointed out, high profile journalists and celebrities continue to focus on rescue missions and media profit from documenting rescue missions and providing the news to their audiences, but the underlying vulnerabilities remain unaddressed.

CONTEMPORARY TRAFFICKING

Historical forms of slavery are easier to identify (today) in terms of exploitative economic, social and political relationships between a slave and his or her master (and mistress), enabled by the states (which legalised slavery) and facilitated by merchants who acquired, bought and sold slaves publicly, and the easily identifiable locations where slaves were held.

If we consider the gamut of trafficking today, as our assumptions and understanding have changed, we now include complex and multifaceted range and forms of human slavery. For example, people are not only trafficked for domestic servitude or bonded or enslaved agriculture labour (along with the associated sexual exploitation) as they were during United States' historical era of formal slavery. Today they are also specifically trafficked for prostitution, beggary, organ removals, bonded labour, and labour in hazardous (industrial) working conditions with minimum wages (Shelley 2010). Organised crime groups are usually involved in long-distance trafficking. Due to the complex and diverse nature of the phenomenon, we cannot, however, simply assume that trafficking is primarily perpetrated by organised criminals. The experiences of victims of trafficking suggest that in majority of the cases either family members or close relatives are involved in the process of trafficking (Raymond 2002; Sanghera 2005; Cameron and Newman 2008). Therefore, Jordan (2001) notes that it is extremely difficult today to identify all traffickers, because depending on the definitions we use, they may include diplomats who import domestic workers to exploit their labour; members of organised criminal networks that transport people transnationally for various forms of exploitation; men who facilitate trafficking of women through forced or fake marriages; and families that exploit men, women, and children to work in homes, offices, agricultural lands, and factories in near-slavery conditions. The enforced movement of these trafficked persons assumes a variety of forms, and, as the last sentence emphasises, there are multiple types of trafficking. As we shall see later, the anti-trafficking interventions do not, however, typically use these expanded conceptualisations of trafficking.

Among factors that lead to trafficking, contemporary scholars point out that traffickers take advantage of vulnerabilities in others, many of which are the outcomes of poverty and poor governance (Sulaimanova 2006). Cameron and Newman (2008) argue that globalisation coupled with liberal economic policies have weakened states' capacities to provide public goods and services. As we discuss later, the primary condition of economic and social vulnerability is enhanced when states comply with structural adjustment pressures from supranational organisations such as the World Bank, and cut back on the supports that would have contributed to addressing the conditions that promote trafficking. Another factor relates to wars and conflicts whose range is enhanced through improved weaponry and rapid sales and distribution of these weapons around the world; these prolonged conflicts create high degrees of economic and social instability and stress among people who are unable to live normal lives. Therefore, trafficking in human beings can be linked to deprivation engendered through contemporary globalisation. Economic and social disparities within and between countries also play crucial roles in determining the flow of internal and transnational trafficking (Purkayastha and Majumdar 2009). Traffickers often prey on individuals who are poor, young, unemployed or underemployed and who may lack access to social safety nets, luring them with stories about opportunities in prosperous areas. Here, too, globalisation plays a part. As Appadurai (1990) argued, cultural globalisation is shaped through rapid dissemination of media reports of conditions elsewhere, the images of consumption and 'good life', and ideologies of modernity. More and more people know and desire such lifestyles. Thus, they are willing to

Figure 2: Reported Human Trafficking: Main Origin, Transit and Destination Countries

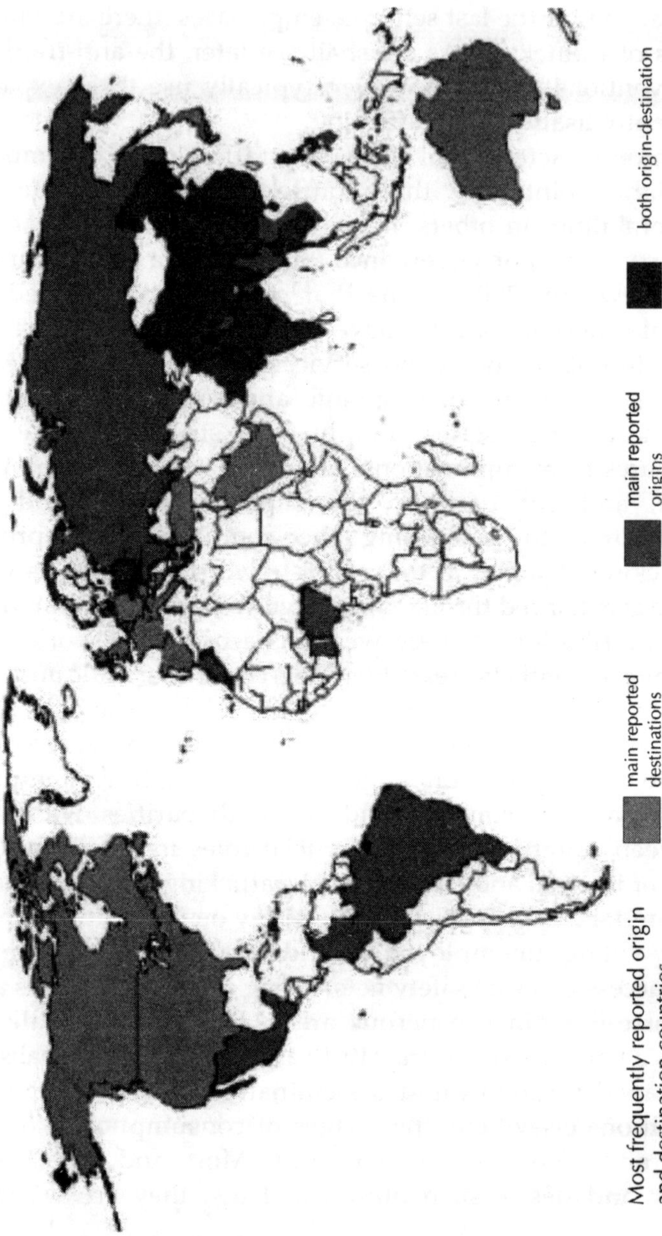

Map Source: United Nations Office on Drugs and Crime (UNODC). 2006. *Trafficking in Persons: Global Patterns.*

follow people who appear to offer opportunities to build better lives. Contemporary globalisation—characterised by highly efficient and speedy networks of communications, image sharing, financial and human networks—has extended the reach of trafficking markets linking people in remote areas with people who buy or benefit from the labour or bodies of the trafficked persons.

Bales (2005) has emphasised the economic processes of modernisation and globalisation that produced devastating effects on the lives of people living in the global South by pushing a substantial number of them into the conditions of social, economic and political vulnerability. The shift from subsistence to market economies has often been accomplished with few intermediate safety nets. People are forced to go to urban areas in search of work while global processes of economic restructuring are undermining job security and social safety nets, especially those provided by states (Naples 2002). The extraction of resources from the global South, through economic restructuring or structural adjustment programmes, has resulted in the destabilisation of many transition economies further intensifying the level of poverty, especially in rural areas (Kara 2011).

The contemporary globalised world economy is hungry for cheap, disposable labour, without much concern about how and where from it comes. This competition leads to situations where the poor, who lack resources and do not find alternate survival opportunities, are trapped and manipulated by traffickers. Many employers exploit low wage labour to compete with others and maximise their profits. Moreover, technological advancements and modern forms of transportation and communication have aided traffickers to easily transfer people within or across countries for exploitation. On one hand, deprived individuals lack power—social, political, and economic—to extricate themselves from the vicious circle of exploitation. On the other hand, traffickers are usually well organised, and easily manage to escape laws (Outshoorn 2005; Cameron and Newman 2008; Kara 2011;

Haerens 2012). For example, Figure 3 clearly shows the inadequacy of existing counter-trafficking mechanisms to prosecute and convict perpetrators of trafficking.

Figure 3: Global Law Enforcement Data

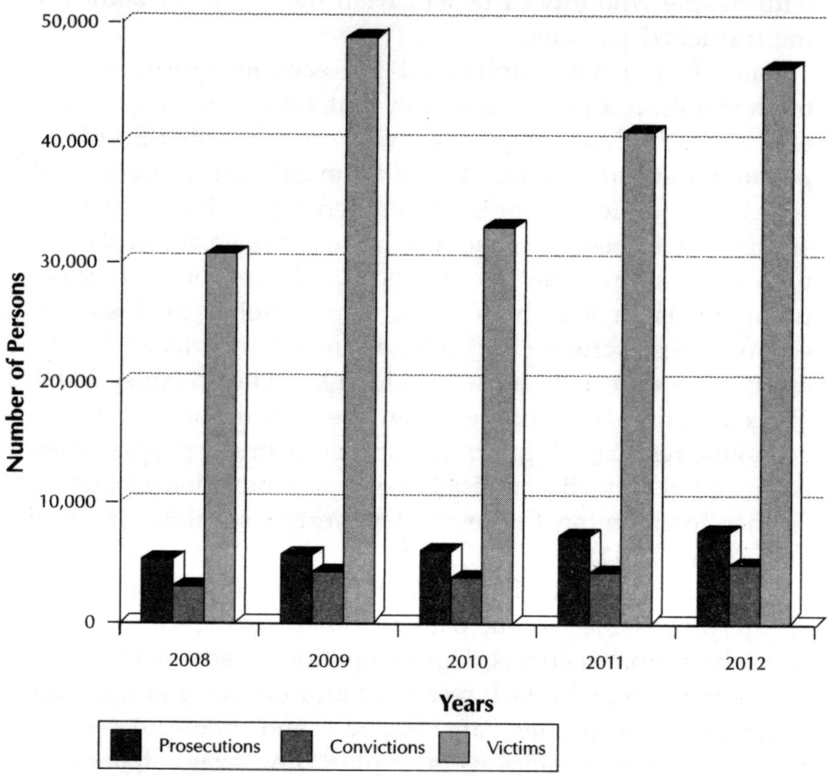

Source: Trafficking in Persons Report 2013

As mentioned earlier, the dramatic increase in the scope and incidences of violence globally act as additional factors that lead to disruption of normal life and create conditions rife for trafficking. At a global level, longitudinal data from the International Peace Research Institute has consistently documented that there have been more deaths in the 20th and 21st centuries from intra-state conflict than inter-state conflict

(Gleditsch *et al.* 2002). Other scholars (e.g., Keegan 1993; Watkin 2004; Fritz, Doering and Gumru 2011) point out that as the mass production of weapons increased dramatically in the 20th century, these concentrated powers of violence among a few countries enabled them to engage in remote wars in distant countries, even as it escalated the range and costs of such wars on ordinary people. These forms of violence and conflict have direct implications on trafficking. When people are caught in situations of prolonged conflict, when their homes and livelihoods are destroyed as 'collateral damage' of large-scale violence, they become vulnerable to trafficking. In situations of economic hardships, especially during or after armed conflicts and natural disasters, the victims are initially lured with false promises of good job opportunities and better lives elsewhere. However, they are later exploited and forced to work under inhuman conditions (Outshoorn 2005; Ebbe 2008; Shelley 2010). Purkayastha and Ratcliff (2014) have also discussed as to how violence unleashed by states to impose 'law and order' in regions within countries can result in large-scale cumulative disruptions of life. Large-scale natural or human made disasters, such as earthquakes or famines, also destroy the fabric of normal life, and without prompt and adequate interventions, entire communities of people become desperate for new opportunities for livelihood and safe shelter. Within these diverse contexts of political, economic, and social instability engendered by conflicts and other disasters, people's vulnerability to trafficking increase; the rapidly weakening provision of social and economic provisions by states under contemporary neo-liberal globalisation further exacerbate the people who are most vulnerable to trafficking.

It is also important to recognise additional political factors that enhance vulnerabilities. Since most countries do not have clear policies on trafficked persons, based on an understanding of the multiple ways in which trafficking occurs, political response to trafficking is often piecemeal. The vulnerability of trafficked persons is significantly enhanced because of the tendency of governments to treat them as criminals or illegal immigrants instead of considering them as human beings possessing rights.[4] Owing to high profits involved in the trade of human beings, and links of traffickers with government officials and politicians, many governments are reluctant to accept the existence of human trafficking in their territories showing hardly any commitment to address the problem (Jordan 2001; Bales 2005; Cameron and Newman 2008; Shelley 2010).

These factors–economic globalisation, political inequities, eroding and changing social support, increasing conflict and violence–structure gender, class, ethnicity, religion, age inequalities to create patterns of vulnerabilities in specific areas. All women are likely to be at far greater risk for sex trafficking than men, but relatively poor, young women are more vulnerable to such exploitation. Existing ideologies that construct ethnically defined groups of women as being more attractive sexually, for instance, stereotypes such as Asian women are said to be mostly willing to do anything to please men (Espiritu 2007), inevitably position these women as profitable trafficked commodities. Similarly, when traffickers seek organs, they tend to turn to middle-aged poverty stricken men who would toil to be good providers for their families.

HOW MANY PEOPLE ARE TRAFFICKED ACROSS THE WORLD?

Owing to complex and clandestine nature of trafficking, it becomes difficult to estimate the actual number of people who are trafficked around the world. Although precise statistics of human trafficking are not available, some anecdotal evidence and studies demonstrate that millions of people are trafficked all over the world annually. Out of them, a disproportionate number of trafficked persons are considered to be women and children. One of the main impediments to estimate the extent of trafficking (discussed in chapter five) is the lack of consensus on what counts as trafficking. Different countries and organisations provide different statistics, based on their particular assumptions about trafficking, implying that available statistics are not reliable for analysing trafficking at cross-country levels. In fact, several organisations provide different estimates of trafficking worldwide (UNESCO 2011). Moreover, the magnitude of trafficking is usually estimated through small-scale surveys which are methodologically weak and cannot be statistically relied upon (Sanghera 2005).

At the time of analysing the data, the very definition of trafficking often leads to quandary. Trafficking is sometimes conflated with illegal migration, smuggling and prostitution too, but from the point of view of scholars, it is not valid to combine illegal or undocumented migration with trafficking because of the element of force and coercion implicit within trafficking. Illegal immigration is often prompted by economic causes or due to wars and conflicts; *some* undocumented migrants are trafficked. Nonetheless, the circumstances and processes of illegal migration can vary based on the openness of the national border, the factors precipitating the migration, and the hardship and distance involved in the process. While trafficking might appear to share these characteristics, a key component of trafficking is that it involves a group or several groups of people who intend to coerce, control and profit from the forced migration of vulnerable individuals. Assumptions about gendered nature of trafficking also play a significant role in determining whether or not trafficking is recognised in a particular context. For example, prostitution may be perceived as a form of trafficking and forced labour in case of girls and women migrants, but not in the case of male migrants (Sanghera 2005; Liempt 2006). So the data on trafficking might only include cases of trafficking of females.

In addition, Bales (2005) notes, if we add forced labour to the data on trafficking, different viewpoints and perceptions of abusive labour practices generate controversy regarding collection, analysis and interpretation of information. For example, some governments are reluctant to admit to the existence of labour exploitation in their territories due to their vested political interests and economic compulsions. Conversely, some NGOs may be interested in claiming the opposite just to get funding from international donors. Bales further notes that owing to the diverse and complicated nature of the issue, a single research strategy to study trafficking may not be the best strategy to analyse diverse forms of trafficking in different parts of the world.

Conducting research on human trafficking is also challenging since it is difficult to access to traffickers and victims as information sources. Victims are often reluctant to share their experiences due to perceived fear of police and/or for fear of stigmatisation if other people come to know how they have been exploited. This is especially true in case of victims of sexual exploitation. According to Sanghera (2005), another key challenge in identifying and dealing with the problem of trafficking is that it is considered a crime only after it has occurred. As trafficking is a process that may involve several stages (e.g., recruitment, transportation, confinement), it is difficult to identify trafficking during its earlier phases.

Likewise, Loff and Sanghera (2004) and Jones (2010) argue that the concept of trafficking still remains confused both conceptually and in practice, which makes its assessment difficult. Some of the factors which enhance this perplexity and make evaluation difficult include: the dominant focus on a subset of trafficked persons (i.e., women and children in sex work); viewing trafficking as a phenomenon that involves coercion, without any agreement or standards on how to define coercion in the complex process of trafficking; failure to differentiate between trafficking in women and trafficking in children, with the concomitant problem of defining the actual limits of childhood; limited education and training of law enforcement agencies and service providers on the issue of human trafficking; limited work with victims and offenders of human trafficking; and, limited inter-organisational collaboration in developing and implementing anti-trafficking interventions.

The Walk Free Foundation which produced a Global Slavery Index (2013) distinguishes between slavery, bonded labour and trafficking. According to them, "'Slavery' refers to the condition of treating another person as if they were property—something to be bought, sold, traded or even destroyed. 'Forced labour' is a related but not identical concept, referring to work taken without consent, by threats or coercion. [Whereas] 'Human trafficking' is another related concept, referring to the process through which people are brought, through deception, threats or coercion, into slavery, forced labour or other forms of severe exploitation" (http://www.globalslaveryindex.org). However, as we will show in the chapter three, these *distinctions* are difficult to sustain for data gathering purposes.

An appreciation of these difficulties of definitions partially explains the problems of gathering data on trafficking. Another practical problem, especially in developing countries like Pakistan, is the lack of infrastructure to constantly gather valid and reliable data on people. As scholars, such as Appadurai (1990), have pointed out, gathering data requires massive state investment in the apparatus of data gathering, collation, storage and analysis. Such infrastructure is not always available, especially in more remote or conflict-torn parts of the country—the exact places that where people vulnerable to trafficking are likely to be located. Furthermore, as most of the people in Pakistan are still unfamiliar with the concept of trafficking, which further interrupts the process of obtaining reliable statistics.

When no official disaggregated statistics of trafficking are available in the country, some organisations tend to provide or quote exaggerated statistics to serve their own interests without revealing any source of information. According to UNESCO (N.d.):

> "When it comes to statistics, trafficking of girls and women is one of several highly emotive issues which seems to overwhelm critical faculties.

> Numbers take on a life of their own, gaining acceptance through repetition, often with little inquiry into their derivations. Journalists, bowing to the pressures of editors, demand numbers, any number. Organisations feel compelled to supply them, lending false precisions and spurious authority to many reports."

In spite of these constraints, all experts agree that the issue of trafficking is widespread and increasing significantly. According to the estimates of TIP Report (2013), based on the information provided by the governments, only around 40,000 victims of trafficking were identified last year. Conversely, several NGOs and social scientists estimate the number of trafficked persons around 27 million. Likewise, the Global Slavery Index Report (2013) notes that there are an estimated 29.8 million people in slavery around the world.

HUMAN TRAFFICKING AND HUMAN SMUGGLING

Due to lack of information and reliable data on human trafficking and its complex nature, the concept of trafficking is usually conflated or used interchangeably with human smuggling (Salt 2000; Loff and Sanghera 2004; Bales 2005; Haque 2006; McCabe and Manian 2010). Although the United Nations Convention on Transnational Organised Crime (2000)[5] and its protocols on trafficking in persons and on migrant smuggling distinguish the two issues, the concept of trafficking in persons is still being intermingled with smuggling of migrants (Konrad 2008). According to Article 3(a) of the Protocol against the Smuggling of Migrants by Land, Sea and Air, Supplementing the United Nations Convention against Transnational Organised Crime, "Smuggling of migrants shall mean the procurement, in order to obtain, directly or indirectly, a financial or other material benefit, of the illegal entry of a person into a State Party of which the person is not a national or a permanent resident". Similarly, the United States

Department of State (2006) notes that "human smuggling is the facilitation, transportation, attempted transportation or illegal entry of a person(s) across an international border, in violation of one or more countries laws, either clandestinely or through deception, such as the use of fraudulent documents (p. 2)". While the key elements of trafficking include threat, use of force or other forms of coercion (abduction, fraud, deception or abuse of power), smuggling generally implies a degree of consent between the smuggler and the person being smuggled (Shelley 2010). Trafficking, on the other hand, implies an absence of such consent, during at least some stage of the trafficking process. However, in the case of trafficked children, the issue of consent is irrelevant.

Like human trafficking, human smuggling is also a global phenomenon that has become a billion-dollar industry and one of the preferred trades for criminal networks across the globe (Kyle and Kolowski 2001). While smuggling involves the movement of person(s) beyond national boundaries, trafficking can take place within or across national boundaries. Moreover, frequently the contract between smugglers and persons being smuggled consists of crossing of international borders through illicit means and the relationship between the contracting parties ends after reaching destination point. Conversely, trafficked persons are deceived or forced into exploitation or slavery-like conditions even after they reach destination point, with or without being smuggled (Icduygu and Toktas 2002; McCabe and Manian 2010).

Here again, though conceptually and legally human trafficking and human smuggling are two distinct processes, in practice, in cases that involve transnational movement, the boundary between smuggling and trafficking becomes blurred. For example, the line is hazy when victims themselves cross international borders illegally or hire the services of smugglers for this purpose; later on they become victims of trafficking at the destination point. This may include cases in which, after reaching point of destination, the smuggled persons are held hostage or forced into exploitative working conditions by the smugglers until the smuggled persons or their families are able to pay off all the expenditures incurred on the process of smuggling. Therefore, it is possible that persons being smuggled may end up as victims of trafficking. Similarly, in some cases women consent to be smuggled to work as prostitutes, lured by fake promise of traffickers of decent working conditions and high wages. But, after reaching the point of destination, traffickers confiscate their documents and force them into slavery-like conditions (Skeldon 2000; Aronowitz 2001; Aronowitz 2002; Bales 2005; Zhang 2007).

It is also crucially important to understand that transnational trafficking may not necessarily involve smuggling or illegal migration. Anderson and Davidson (2003) note that some individuals who become victims of trafficking make a free choice to migrate legally; later on, they are subject to trafficking. For example, some women may legally migrate as wives and then be subjected to forced labour or sexual exploitation. Frequently, owing to corruption of government officials and poor enforcement of laws, traffickers abuse the vulnerability of economically weaker migrants and push them into the conditions of labour exploitation and hazardous working environment.

Despite some common features, human trafficking is distinctly different from human smuggling and requires specific interventions for prosecution, protection, and prevention (Liempt 2006; Konrad 2008). Persons being smuggled violate immigration laws, whereas trafficked persons are victims of exploitation whose rights have been violated. However, frequently the response of law enforcement agencies has been treating the victims of trafficking same as persons involved in smuggling, with efforts focused on their immediate deportation.

Thus, the response based on incomplete understanding of trafficking may result in denying rights to the trafficked persons. For example, in case of Pakistan, the situation becomes more problematic as the term 'trafficking' is frequently translated into Urdu language as 'smuggling' for this is how trafficking is widely known or reported. In addition, trafficking laws in Pakistan do not differentiate trafficking and smuggling, which further enhance the confusion in understanding how trafficking is different from smuggling. As a result, law enforcement agencies tend to report human smuggling, illegal migration, and trafficking together under the same law (Hussein and Hussain 2012; TIP Report 2013). Moreover, as the trafficking legislation in Pakistan defines trafficking as a process that involves movement into or out of the country, it means persons who are trafficked internally are deprived of receiving the state protection and support under trafficking laws.

CHAPTER 2
Human Trafficking: A Focus on South Asia and Pakistan

Even though this critique focuses particularly on Pakistan, we begin this chapter with an overview of human trafficking in South Asia. This larger context is important because trafficking does not respect political boundaries. Depending on the power of a trafficking organisation, especially in the mountainous regions of South Asia, trafficking is rarely contained in single countries. Second, the South Asian countries have developed some levels of co-operation and edifices of laws and practices on trafficking that could, at least theoretically, be shared among the countries. All of the South Asian countries have conditions—economic, political, socio-cultural—that make people vulnerable to trafficking; while each country's specificities matter in terms of the victims' experiences, from the vantage point of studying this topic, it is interesting to position Pakistan within this regional landscape of trafficking. Following this regional background, we provide an overview of the prevalence of human trafficking in Pakistan and highlight the intensity of the factors (we described in the previous chapter) as a prologue to our discussion on trafficking.

HUMAN TRAFFICKING IN SOUTH ASIA

According to the estimates of United Nations Development Programme (2007), South Asia[6] has the second largest number of internationally trafficked persons in the world, and overall, 150,000-200,000 people from the region are trafficked annually. Although people are trafficked to and from South Asia across the world, the majority of them are trafficked either within the countries of the region or to the Middle East (Yousaf 2006; UNODC 2007). Purkyastha and Majumdar (2009) note two major reasons that facilitate trafficking within the region. First, owing to cultural similarities between the countries of the region, which share much of the cultural pluralism, it becomes difficult to identify victims of trafficking based on the common perception of foreignness (e.g., language, phenotype). Second, porous borders, in some sections of the region, make the movement of people easier from one country to another. Many countries in South Asia are used as origin, transit, and destination point for trafficking.

While Bangladesh, Nepal, and Sri Lanka are primary countries of origin, India and Pakistan are main countries of destination or transit to other countries (Asian Development Bank 2003; UNODC 2007). In South Asia, due to inadequate understanding of human trafficking and smuggling, lack of capacity on part of the government agencies and narrow scope of trafficking laws coupled with frail enforcement mechanism, only a small proportion of trafficked persons are recognised as victims of trafficking by the governments, and consequently are provided with protection and rehabilitation support. In the majority of cases, officials of law enforcement agencies require victims of trafficking to provide 'sufficient proof' of being 'forced into trafficking' failing which they are treated as criminals (UNODC 2007; Hukil 2013). Moreover, despite trafficking of large number of men in the region, especially into forced labour, debt bondage, and organ trade, like many other parts of the world, the phenomenon of trafficking is associated with women only. Hence, there is hardly any data or information available regarding nature of trafficking of men in the region (Masud Ali 2005; Hukil 2013).

The South Asian region is marked by various forms of social-political-economic inequalities. The region is home to

Figure 4: Reported Trafficking in Asia

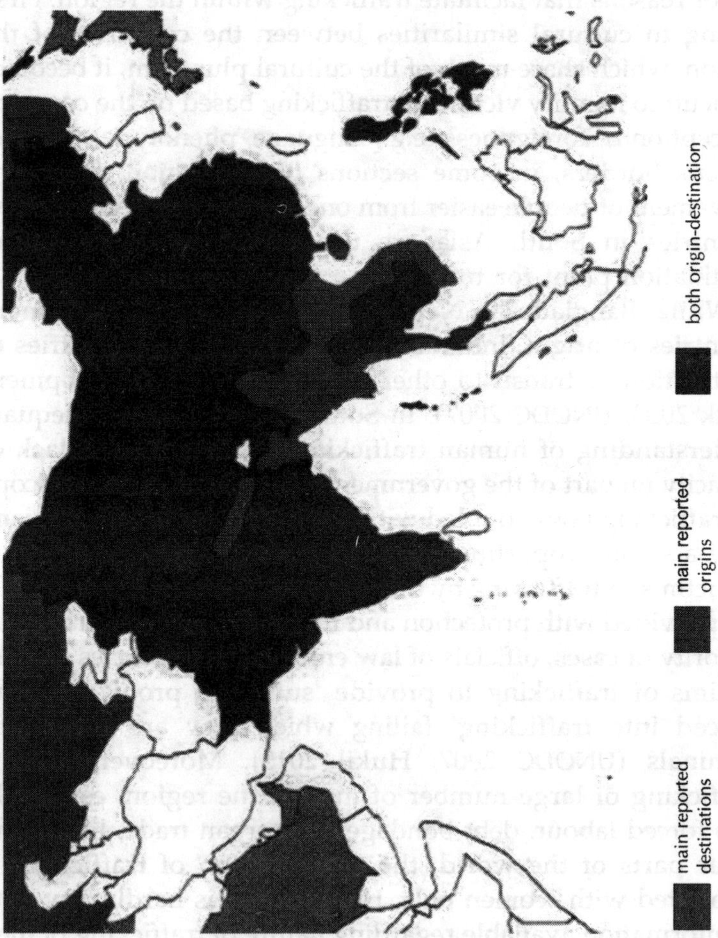

Map Source: UNODC. 2006. *Trafficking in Persons: Global Patterns.*

more than one-fifth of the world's population, of which more than thirty five per cent of people live under the conditions of poverty. Owing to the existence of intense poverty, instable economic conditions, deteriorating security systems, and weak law enforcement in the region, many children and adults are exposed to great risk of being trafficked into sex industry, forced marriages, organ removal and different forms of forced labour (UNDP 2007; Shelly 2010; Hukil 2013). Rapid commercialisation of agriculture land and decline in productivity together with environmental erosion and natural disasters are leading to loss of traditional livelihoods without alternate options, which further enhance the vulnerability of women, children and men to exploitation (Asian Development Bank 2003).

Although people are trafficked into diverse forms of exploitation, trafficking in women and girls for commercial sexual exploitation is the most widespread form in South Asia (UNODC 2007). According to Purkyastha and Majumdar (2009:3), the main contributing factors to sex trafficking in the region include "the impoverishment of groups especially through Structural Adjustment Programmes (SAPs), the rapid growth of feminised jobs and the lure of these 'well paid' jobs for women in impoverished areas, easier access to long distance travel, the circulating global imageries via global media of life in other places that attract women who want to move to these 'familiar places' in order to create better lives for themselves, disruptions and social disorder introduced by war and prolonged violent conflict, and the racial commoditisation and marketing of women's bodies".

Moreover, trafficking in women and girls for commercial sexual exploitation in South Asia has some serious public health implications, especially in terms of strong links between trafficking and Sexually Transmitted Infections (STIs) and dispersion of HIV/AIDS (UNDP 2003; Dickenson 2006; Huda 2006; Brysk 2009; Birkenthal 2011). For example, a study of commercial sex markets in Nepal demonstrates that trafficked women have significantly higher risk of contracting HIV than non-trafficked women (UNODC 2008). Due to rapid growth in HIV/AIDS, the region has become home to high concentration of people living with HIV/AIDS with an estimated more than 5 million HIV-positive people (Zakar 2004; Huda 2006; UNODC 2008). In South Asia, trafficking in young girls for sexual exploitation is high in demand because of the myth that sex with a virgin can cure STIs and HIV/AIDS and the perception that young girls have less chances of carrying STIs and HIV/AIDS (Asian Development Bank 2003). The young girls who are trafficked for sexual exploitation face an enormous risk of HIV/AIDS on account of lack of control over their working and living conditions, including lack of power to negotiate use of condoms in sexual relations. As a result, they become main drivers of the epidemic (UNDP 2007). Despite the fact that aggravating links between trafficking and HIV/AIDS pose serious challenges to the whole region of South Asia, the response of the states has been weak at best. It is important to note that six countries of the region, including Pakistan, Bangladesh, Nepal, Afghanistan, Bhutan, Maldives, and Nepal have not yet signed the UN Protocol to Prevent, Suppress and Punish Trafficking in Persons.

STATES' RESPONSE TO TRAFFICKING IN SOUTH ASIA

Before we turn to Pakistan, it is important to show how the other South Asian countries define and respond to trafficking. The TIP Report (2013) provides country narratives that briefly explain the nature and magnitude of trafficking in each country and the efforts of the government to combat trafficking. Based on the evaluation of progress made by the countries to counter trafficking over the last one year, they are ranked on 3-tier system. According to the TIP Report (2013:55), explanation of different Tiers is as under:

- TIER 1: Countries whose governments fully comply with the TVPA's (Trafficking Victims Protection Act) minimum standards.

- TIER 2: Countries whose governments do not fully comply with the TVPA's minimum standards, but are making significant efforts to bring themselves into compliance with those standards.

- TIER 2 SPECIAL WATCH LIST: Countries whose governments do not fully comply with the TVPA's minimum standards but are making significant efforts to bring themselves into compliance with those standards, AND:
  a) The absolute number of victims of severe forms of trafficking is very significant or is significantly increasing;
  b) There is a failure to provide evidence of increasing efforts to combat severe forms of trafficking in persons from the previous year; or
  c) The determination that a country is making significant efforts to bring itself into compliance with minimum standards was based on commitments by the country to take additional future steps over the next year.

- TIER 3: Countries whose governments do not fully comply with the TVPA's minimum standards and are not making significant efforts to do so.

As the states in South Asia have not yet taken adequate measures to control the menace of human trafficking in the region, India, Pakistan, Bangladesh, Nepal, and Bhutan are placed under Tier 2, whereas Afghanistan, Sri Lanka and Maldives are ranked in Tier 2 Watch List. Further, drawing upon information provided in the TIP Report (2013), in this section, we briefly discuss the states' response to trafficking in South Asia.

Afghanistan

Afghanistan is a source, transit and destination country in terms of trafficking in women, men and children mainly for sexual exploitation and forced labour. The majority of trafficked persons in Afghanistan comprise children who are subject to exploitation and slavery-like conditions in sectors such as carpet weaving, brick kiln factories, domestic servitude, commercial sexual exploitation and smuggling of narcotics and drugs within Afghanistan and in Pakistan, Iran and Saudi Arabia. Women and girls from neighbouring countries are also trafficked to Afghanistan for prostitution. Due to lack of understanding of trafficking, the government agencies tend to further victimise the victims of trafficking for offenses committed in the course of being trafficked. Moreover, human trafficking is frequently conflated with human smuggling because in the local language same word is used to refer to both human trafficking and human smuggling. Although Afghanistan's Countering Abduction and Human Trafficking/Smuggling Law (2008) prohibits trafficking in persons and prescribes penalties for those who are involved in perpetrating trafficking, the narrow scope of the law focuses on only certain forms of trafficking. As the Government of Afghanistan does not fully comply with the minimum standards for eliminating trafficking and has not yet taken significant counter-trafficking steps to improve the situation, the country is placed on Tier 2 Watch List.

Bangladesh

Bangladesh is mainly a source country for trafficking in women, men and children for forced labour and sexual exploitation. The Human Trafficking and Deterrence and Suppression Act (HTDSA) and the National Plan of Action (2012-2014) for Combating Human Trafficking are considered the most significant initiatives of the government to address the issue of human trafficking. According to the HTDSA, human trafficking is defined as "The selling, buying, recruitment, receipt, transportation, transfer, or harbouring of any person for the purpose of sexual-exploitation, labour-exploitation or any other form of exploitation whether in or outside of Bangladesh by means of (a) threat or use of force or other forms of coercion, or (b) abduction, fraud or deception, or of the abuse of any person's socio-economic, environmental or other types of vulnerability, or (c) of the giving or receiving of payments or benefits to achieve the consent of a person having control over another person" (Ministry of Home Affairs, Government of the People's Republic of Bangladesh 2012: 12). Owing to weak mechanisms of law enforcement, Bangladesh, however, continues to be a recruiting point for trafficking in persons. Moreover, the government has made few efforts to protect victims of trafficking, especially in terms of identifying victims of trafficking and providing them shelter and other services. Bangladesh is placed on Tier 2 because it does not fully comply with the minimum standards for the elimination of trafficking, but it is making significant efforts to do so.

Bhutan

Bhutan, a small mountainous country positioned between India and Nepal, is mainly a destination country for trafficking in men, women and children for forced labour and sexual exploitation. According to the Penal Code (Amendment) Act of Bhutan (2011),[7] amended Section 154, "A defendant shall be guilty of the offence of trafficking a person if the defendant recruits, transports, sells or buys, harbours or receives a person through the use of threat or force or deception within, into or outside of Bhutan for any illegal purpose". In Bhutan, as it is evident from this definition, trafficking is considered as a crime that is conducted for any illegal purpose rather than exploitation of human beings. Due to the lack of capacity of government agencies and limited understanding of the phenomenon, cases of trafficking are frequently not identified properly. The government provides protection to victims of trafficking, including shelter and other services, through a government-funded NGO. However, such services are only available for trafficked women and children. Bhutan is placed on Tier 2 because it does not fully comply with the minimum standards for the elimination of trafficking; it has, however, taken significant initiatives towards eradication of trafficking.

India

India is a source, transit, and destination country for trafficking in men, women and children. In India, people are trafficked mainly for forced labour, debt bondage and sexual exploitation. The main issue in the country is internal trafficking as most of the cases involve trafficking of Indians within Indian states, though Nepalis and Bangladeshis are trafficked to India too. In addition to the Immoral Traffic (Prevention) Act that prohibits trafficking in persons, the penal code was amended in 2013 through adoption of the Criminal Law Amendments Act to broaden the scope of the definition of trafficking and prescribe more stringent punishments for trafficking related crimes. Due to inadequate law enforcement mechanism and lack of understanding of trafficking, victims of trafficking are, however, frequently further victimised by law enforcement agencies. In addition, due to lack of funding, shelters for victims of trafficking, run by the government and NGOs, do not provide adequate services. India is placed on Tier 2 because the government does not fully comply with the minimum standards for the elimination of trafficking; however, it is taking significant steps to counter trafficking.

Maldives

Maldives is mainly a destination country in terms of trafficking in women, men and children for forced labour and sexual exploitation. Due to lack of understanding of the issue, trafficking is generally conflated with human smuggling. As a result, anti-trafficking interventions focus on illegal or undocumented migration only. Moreover, the government lacks systematic mechanism to identify victims of trafficking and to provide them protective services. Owing to these institutional constraints, many victims of trafficking are subject to further victimisation. Maldives does not have adequate legislation to deal with all types of human trafficking. As the Government of Maldives does not fully comply with the minimum standards for the elimination of trafficking, the country is placed on Tier 2 Watch List.

Nepal

Nepal is a source, transit and destination country for trafficking in men, women and children. In Nepal, people are trafficked mainly for forced labour and sexual exploitation. According to the Human Trafficking and Transportation (Control) Act of 2007,[8] "If anyone commits any of the following acts, that shall be deemed to have committed human trafficking: (a) To sell or purchase a person for any purpose, (b) To use someone into prostitution, with or without any benefit, (c) To extract human organ except otherwise determined by law, (d) To go for in prostitution". Owing to weak law enforcement mechanism and limited understanding of government officials regarding the concept of trafficking, many victims of trafficking are re-victimised. Nepal is placed on Tier 2 because the government does not fully comply with the minimum standards for the elimination of trafficking; however, significant efforts are being made to do so.

Sri Lanka

Sri Lanka is mainly a source country in terms of trafficking in women, men and children for forced labour and sexual exploitation. According to the Penal Code of Sri Lanka (as amended in 2006),[9] "Whoever—(a) buys, sells or barters or instigates another person to buy, sell or barter any person or does anything to promote, facilitate or induce the buying, selling or bartering of any person for money or other consideration; (b) recruits, transports, transfers, harbours or receives any person or does any other act by the use of threat, force, fraud, deception or inducement or by exploiting the vulnerability of another for the purpose of securing forced or compulsory labour or services, slavery, servitude, the removal of organs, prostitution or other forms of sexual exploitation or any other act which constitutes an offence under any law; (c) recruits, transports, transfers, harbours or receives a child or does any other act whether with or without the consent of such child for the purpose of securing forced or compulsory labour or services, slavery, servitude or the removal of organs, prostitution or other forms of sexual exploitation, or any other act which constitutes an offence under any law, shall be guilty of the offence of trafficking". Due to limited understanding of trafficking and lack of capacity of government officials, trafficking is usually confused with other crimes, including human smuggling, illegal migration and prostitution. As a result, there is a weak mechanism to identify victims of trafficking, which results in re-victimisation of trafficked persons. Sri Lanka is placed on Tier 2 Watch List because the government does not comply with the minimum standards for the elimination of trafficking.

Thus, it is clear that the definitions of trafficking vary among the countries. However, it is important to note that several South Asian countries proscribe against labour trafficking and the trade in human organs, a theme that does not always receive the deserved attention in the *international* discourse on trafficking.

SAARC: PATTERNS OF COOPERATION AND COMPLIANCE WITH ANTI-TRAFFICKING PRINCIPLES

Besides country specific trafficking legislations, all countries of the region have ratified the South Asian Association for Regional Cooperation (SAARC)[10] Convention on Prevention and Combating Trafficking in Women and Children for Prostitution (2002) that came into force in November 2005. Due to limited scope of the Convention (discussed in chapter five), lack of coordination among border security and law enforcing agencies of the region, and failure of the governments to harmonise their national anti-trafficking policies, the problem of trafficking in South Asia largely remains unaddressed. Moreover, long prevailing traditional political problems and conflicts between countries of the region make it even more difficult to develop and implement a joint strategy to curb the menace of trafficking at the regional level. As a result, anti-trafficking activities in the region are mainly initiated by NGOs and International organisations, especially in terms of providing shelter, health and legal assistance to victims of trafficking (Yousaf 2006; UNODC 2007; Hukil 2013). The strong linkage between the local NGOs and international organisations, to some extent, has been successful in combating trafficking and shaping response to trafficking as an issue of human rights violations (Purkayastha and Majumdar 2009).

HUMAN TRAFFICKING IN PAKISTAN: A BRIEF OVERVIEW OF THE PROBLEM

Pakistan is a destination point for persons who are trafficked in from Bangladesh, Myanmar, Afghanistan and Central Asia. The country is a transit point for those brought in from East Asia and Bangladesh to be taken elsewhere. It is also a recruiting ground for those who are internally (inter-provincially) trafficked or sent to Afghanistan and the Gulf (Huda 2006; Shelley 2010; TIP Report 2013). Due to lack of understanding about the issue of human trafficking in Pakistan, no official data are available for the country. Some of the main reasons for not consolidating trafficking related data in Pakistan include the following: cases of trafficking, especially of internal trafficking, are frequently not reported or identified as trafficking; even when trafficking cases are reported, they are generally registered under other offences which are not consolidated as trafficking related crimes; many cases of internal trafficking are associated with traditional practices (e.g., trade of women to settle disputes), which are not considered as trafficking; due to multifaceted and clandestine nature of trafficking, it is, therefore, difficult to assess the magnitude of human trafficking in Pakistan based on small scale surveys or anecdotal studies (Hussein and Hussain 2012).

Despite the paucity of government data, various international organisations and NGOs provide valuable information regarding nature and extent of trafficking in Pakistan. According to the Global Slavery Index Report (2013), Pakistan is third on the Index in terms of the highest prevalence of modern slavery, with an estimated 20,00,000 to 22,00,000 people subject to various forms of slavery. In the absence of statistics on trafficking specifically, these data on slavery—developed from estimates for three indices, including trafficking, which are then combined to create the slavery index—provide some indication of dimension of extreme vulnerability among people in the country.

Awan and Brohi (2000) note that the first case of human trafficking in Pakistan was reported in early 1980s when several Bangladeshi women were found imprisoned in Karachi. Upon investigation, it was revealed that the women were recruited in Bangladesh by traffickers through false promises of better job opportunities and quality of life, and were trafficked to Pakistan using illicit means. Likewise, several estimates indicate that during the last decade of the 20th century, 200,000 women and girls between the ages of 12 and 30 years were trafficked from Bangladesh to Pakistan (Lawyers for Human Rights and Legal Aid 1996; Awan and Brohi 2000; Jalalzai 2002; Yousaf 2006). It is estimated that on an average 100 to 150 women enter Pakistan daily through illicit means and very few of them ever return to their homes (Sarwar 1997; Haider 2005). Girls and women from rural areas of Pakistan are also trafficked to urban centres for commercial sexual exploitation and labour. Moreover, Pakistan had been a main country of origin for trafficking of thousands of children to the United Arab Emirates to work as camel jockeys. Over the last few years, enactment of laws prohibiting child camel jockeys in the United Arab Emirates and concentrated efforts of Pakistan have, however, significantly reduced the number of boys trafficked through Pakistan for that purpose (Haider 2005; Huda 2006).

According to the TIP Report (2013), Pakistan is placed under the Tier 2 as the Government of Pakistan does not fully comply with the minimum standards for the elimination of human trafficking; however, it is making significant efforts in this direction. The report also highlights that concerned agencies in the country do not have any systematic methods of identifying victims of trafficking and referring them to protective services.

POLITICAL AND ECONOMIC INSTABILITY

In countries which are affected by long periods of instability, like Pakistan, in the context of this study, the nature of political and economic instability, including the international structures that shape such conflicts are important factors for understanding trafficking. Political instability and conflicts enhance the vulnerability of people, especially the disadvantaged groups, to trafficking (Outshoorn 2005; Ebbe 2008; Shelley 2010). Pakistan has been a close ally of the West initially during the Cold War and later on in the War on Terrorism. During the Cold War period, massive funding was provided by the United States to the military regime in Pakistan to train and support militant groups to counter the Soviets in Afghanistan. This was one of the main contributing factors that led to the emergence of radical religious movements and extremism in Pakistan which had have devastating effects on the society—politically, socially, and economically (Critelli 2010). Weak economy coupled with deteriorating law and order situation contribute significantly to increase in number of people who are subject to trafficking or slavery-like conditions in Pakistan (Global Slavery Index 2013). Moreover, the ongoing conflicts within and among many countries of South Asia (e.g., hostility and wars between Pakistan and India, war in Afghanistan) contribute to social dislocation and increased vulnerability of individuals to trafficking (Purkayastha and Majumdar 2009). In addition, as human trafficking is a high-profit criminal activity, it may have links with other criminal activities, for example, with illegal trade of arms, narcotics, and funding terrorism (Skeldon 2000; Bales 2005). Also, the TIP Report (2013) notes that in some cases militant groups in Pakistan and Afghanistan resort to trafficking children to use them for terrorist activities (e.g., suicide bombing).

Over the last decade, growing extremism and deteriorating law and order situation—within the country and in the region—have been the prime concern for the Government of Pakistan. Consequently, national security, instead of human security, has become the main focus of the state. The bulk of resources are allocated for activities deemed important to national security, for example, military spending and borders security. In this situation, provision of social services or social safety nets for vulnerable population becomes significance of secondary importance for the government with fragile economy and scarce financial resources. These conditions also make Pakistan an 'attractive client' for global financial institutions for loans and grants, tied with strings in the shape of structural adjustment programmes, which further produce devastating effects on the lives of poor. Consequently, many segments of population, especially women, children and those living in rural areas, are unable to receive enough resources even to meet their basic needs (e.g., food, education, health) and become exposed to trafficking.

Vulnerability to trafficking is significantly enhanced when people are displaced from their traditional communities by natural or man-made disasters and conflicts. The Internally Displaced Person (IDP) Vulnerability Assessment & Profiling Project (IVAP),[11] initiated in 2010, provides some data on off-camp conflict-IDPs in north-west Pakistan. Due to long prevailing armed conflicts and military operation against militants in this area, many families had been forced to leave their conflict-affected communities. The data of IVAP, collected from 81, 809 families, show multiple vulnerabilities of the IDP families who lack access to basic services including health, food, secure shelter and livelihood. As a result, many IDP families are inclined towards negative coping strategies (e.g., purchasing food on debt or borrowing food, decrease in expenditure on health and education of children, skipping meals). A significant proportion of the IDP families (approximately 36%), identified by the IVAP, are not officially recognised as IDPs because they do not meet the government's registration criteria. The two main eligibility criteria of the government to register a family as an IDP family include: (a) the family must originate from a government declared 'notified' (conflict affected) area; and, (b) the family must have a Computerised National Identity Card. Only those families that meet the "eligibility criteria" are registered and receive formal assistance packages. Obviously, this approach to register IDPs not only excludes many off-camp families to receive official assistance as IDPs, but also makes them a very high-risk population for internal and transnational trafficking.

In addition, due to political unrest and armed conflicts in the neighbouring country Afghanistan, Pakistan continues to host one of the highest numbers of refugees worldwide. Despite the efforts of the United Nations High Commissioner for Refugees (UNHCR) that has facilitated the return of 3.8 million registered Afghan refugees from Pakistan since 2002, still it is estimated that there are more than 1.6 million Afghan refugees in the country (UNHCR 2014). Refugees who are uprooted from their traditional societies and have lost their livelihoods often become dependent on foreign aid (Shelley 2010). Owing to their multiple vulnerabilities, the refugees also become one of the main targets of trafficking and other forms of exploitation. According to Wilson (2012), the main factors that increase trafficking risks for refugees include: physical insecurity; social, economic, and political marginalisation; disruption of family structure; sexual violence; and lack of legal protection. Moreover, due to long prevailing armed conflicts in Afghanistan, there has been a continuing social disorganisation in the country. As a result, the country shows high levels of unemployment, tall proportions of transient populations, low-income levels, poverty and high rates of migration (Bush 2010). Not surprisingly, conflict prone and poverty stricken areas in Afghanistan have become origin of trafficking in women and children to Pakistan and some other countries, especially for domestic servitude and sexual exploitation (TIP Report 2013).

Similar accounts of sexual exploitation are beginning to emerge from other zones of political conflict (e.g., Njiru & Purkayastha 2014). Moreover, women who are trafficked from zones of political conflict to other countries, especially for sexual exploitation, are reluctant to approach authorities because of the fear they would be treated as illegal immigrants involved in prostitution (Cameron and Newman 2008).

The next chapter illustrates some of these facets of trafficking from the perspective of victims.

CHAPTER 3
Gender and Human Trafficking

Since several estimates of trafficking suggest that the vast majority of trafficked persons in the world are women and girls, in the minds of many activists, donors and policy makers, human trafficking is a gendered phenomenon. The estimates also show that the most exploitative forms of trafficking relate to trafficking of women and children for purposes such as commercial sex work, domestic servitude and child labour of all forms (Bales 2004; Batstone 2007; Brysk 2009; Segrave, Milivojevic and Pickering 2009; Holmes 2010; Shelly 2010).

When gender and trafficking are discussed, most scholars continue to focus on women. Moving away from this approach, we use an intersectional approach to understand trafficking of women, girls, and men within a broader context of exploitation and violence. We not only consider gender—the structured inequalities that result in hierarchies between men and women—we also consider how gender intersects with other structures of inequality such as class or age (Collins 2009; Sinha and Dasgupta 2009; Purkayastha 2010). We draw on the current theoretical approaches that point out not all women or men have same life experiences (Connell 1985; Collins 2009; Hua and Nigorizawa 2010; Hua 2011). Since gendered vulnerabilities are shaped through intersecting social locations structured through class positions, age, race and/or ethnicity, nationality, sexuality, geographical location, religion, exactly which men or women are more likely to be vulnerable to trafficking is ultimately a reflection of stratifications within a society, and that society's position within a global political-economic order. In the last chapter, we described the uneven terrain of anti-trafficking initiatives in the SAARC countries. These differences in responses contribute to the diverse contexts for trafficking too. Traffickers are able to target more internally displaced persons in countries where such camps exist. Traffickers are able to sell women and children for sex trafficking or domestic servitude where markets for these human beings exist. Traffickers are able to target men who are held in bondage for their labour to sell their organs to organisations that are well positioned in that country to sell organs in a local or global market.

As the next sections show, Pakistan is a receiving country for trafficked people from war-torn Afghanistan and economically distressed parts of Bangladesh. The victims often endure multiple episodes of trafficking, remaining beneath the radar of the anti-trafficking laws and policies in place currently.

TRAFFICKING AND PROSTITUTION

Much of the literature on sex trafficking has focused on women and girls who are sold into prostitution. Many of the accounts describe how these victims are held in near-slavery conditions, as sex slaves, in brothels (Grant 2014). However, the emphasis on prostitution has made non-commercial, episodic prostitution—not by choice but through coercion—relatively invisible. Similarly, accounts of forced marriages where women and girls are forced into domestic and sexual servitude are not often part of the discussion on trafficking. The next few accounts, composites created from victims' narratives, show the continuum of coercion and violence and the blurred zone for defining what is trafficking (i.e., a crime by human rights standards) and what is a cultural practice (i.e., part of 'normal' life) or what is slavery vs bonded labour vs trafficking as we discussed in chapter 2.

FORCED MARRIAGE/FORCED LABOUR: BRINGING HOMES BACK TO THE DISCUSSION ON TRAFFICKING

In order to emphasise some points we made in chapter one—the need to consider a continuum of violence as well as considering forced labour wherever it occurs—we start with "Salma's" account. She was interviewed in a shelter after she had been there a couple of weeks.

> After passing the matriculation exams [tenth grade], I really wanted to go to college for higher education to earn a better future. But, my family decided that I had already gotten enough education, and I should perform household chores instead of wasting time in education. Few months ago, in order to resolve a dispute relating to property, I was forced by the elders of my family to marry a boy who was just 16 years old, uneducated, and was not doing any work. Nobody even asked about my consent to marry that boy. After marriage, I became a domestic servant. Despite the fact that I worked continuously from early morning till night, nobody would ever treat me as a human. I was treated as a purchased slave. Frequently, I was physically abused by my husband and his family members. I informed my family [parents] about this situation, but they told me that I might die there but should not ever think to return to them. I ran away from home and came to the shelter. I don't know where to go and what will happen to me in future.
>
> (a victim of trafficking, age 22 years)

We begin by featuring Salma's account because in some ways she does not appear to be the quintessential marginalised woman who is often featured in media accounts—i.e., the woman who was sold to a brothel and would have a different chance of life if only she had earned an education. Salma matriculated from high school, so she is better off than women who yearn for education. Nonetheless, the factors that increase their vulnerability are the intersecting gendered norms about the limits to women's education and the acceptance of women as currency for settling disputes along with the structures that position *young* unmarried and married women in powerless positions, as 'purchased slave[s]' within households. However, the larger structural barriers, Salma's lack of options about challenging violence—since her family condones the violence—and her dejection about the lack of options beyond the shelter are important elements of her narrative.

While most of the trafficking literature focuses on the close connection between trafficking and prostitution, we argue that such extreme control and exploitation for labour need to be considered as part of the continuum of trafficking. By her own account, Salma comes closest to indentured labour because she has no options to resist or change the situation in which she finds herself. She experiences violence. Her marriage implicitly involves an exchange that includes provisions for sex (within the meaning of forced marriage) even though she does not mention it herself.

Furthermore, Salma's case points to another aspect of trafficking. Women like Salma normally would not be on the radar as people discuss trafficking, since the term assumes there is profit to be made. Usually the emphasis is on *material profit* alone whereas in social exchange the woman is a mere currency involving a form of exchange *and profit*. Here we draw upon decades of feminist literature that has demonstrated the material contributions of women who perform domestic labour throughout their life significantly subsidising the material resources of any household since the replacement of their labour is often prohibitively expensive (see e.g., Purkayastha *et al.* 2012 for a summary). The gendered ideologies that frame women's domestic labour in the private sphere as 'labour of love' and societies that do not recognise such work through formal social benefits contribute centrally to the economic and social inequalities between 'non-working women' and 'working men or women' and constrain their choices in life. Salma's work as a 'domestic servant' or 'purchased slave' contributes to the material well-being of the marital household; consequently, this young woman's work is profitable for the household *and* society. Yet at the micro level, her domestic service yields nothing for her. Even what is more important, from her perspective, married or not, is the outcome of both families' treatment of her is similar to people who are enslaved. And, as we discuss later, her lack of options beyond the shelter, exacerbate her vulnerability to trafficking for direct monetary profit later. Moving beyond Salma's case, it is important to note that in Pakistan, women have been particularly vulnerable to exploitation and trafficking largely due to such persistent gender inequalities in every sphere of life. Family is generally considered as a private matter where state is not supposed to intervene. In addition, in some areas of Pakistan, tribal/feudal lords and the male dominated institution of *jirga/panchayat* (informal justice system) sanction the exploitation of women in the name of traditional practices. These conventional discriminatory practices that subjugate women and enable their commodification are significant contributing factors leading to the exploitation of women and girls (Awan and Brohi 2000; Haider 2005; Hussein and Hussain 2012).

Furthermore, widespread gender inequalities and low status of women multiply their vulnerability to trafficking for they have fewer options or available resources to counter the deception of traffickers. As Saeed (2002) has pointed out, stereotypical gendered socialisation of men and women reinforce a sense of women's helplessness and of being unprotected without a man. In addition, women and girls are most likely to suffer from stigmatisation if and when they return to their natal homes and communities especially after experiencing sexual exploitation. Thus, they have fewer options for alternative survival strategies. Likewise, the fear of stigmatisation and further victimisation by police help traffickers increasing their control over trafficked women (Asian Development Bank 2003).

TRAFFICKING AND PROSTITUTION

Since the emergence of the term trafficking, the dominant focus of discussions about trafficking has been on trafficking for sexual exploitation and prostitution. The literature on this subject originates from two opposite feminist perspectives: 'women as victims' and 'women exercising agency and choice' (Bertone 2000; Doezema 2002; Jeffreys 2003; Chew 2006; Zheng 2010). The first perspective opposes the legalisation of prostitution and argues that prostitution can never be a voluntary occupation because it always involves elements of force, deception and coercion. Whereas the second perspective promotes the legalisation of prostitution and argues that stigmatisation of prostitution is a form of patriarchal control over women, and legalisation of prostitution will restore women's agency and control over their own bodies. Similarly, two leading international NGOs, including Global Alliance Against Traffic in Women (GAATW) and Coalition Against Trafficking Women (CATW), both part of the anti-trafficking movement, also represent these two opposing views. While the CATW supports illegalising prostitution as an effective way to combat trafficking, the GAATW argues that formalising prostitution can reduce trafficking because it is the illicit nature of this profession that increases the women's vulnerability to exploitation.

Some scholars (e.g., Sietske 1995; Gould 2001; Doezema 2002; Thorbek 2002) challenge the assumption that women's consent to undertake sex work is meaningless and argue that not all prostitutes are victims of trafficking or sex slave. For example, some sex workers consider their work to be just like other forms of labour, and not necessarily involve exploitation or subjugation. Women's agency to make choices about their own bodies cannot be ignored; therefore, whether a woman engages in sex work through free choice remains an empirical question. Prevalent ideologies and abolitionist laws help stigmatise sex workers and further increase their vulnerability to exploitation by preventing them from forming unions to claim and protect their rights as workers.

Moreover, many scholars place trafficking for sexual exploitation within a global political economy that produces gendered power inequalities and vulnerabilities. Sinha and Dasgupta (2009) argue that the factors of class, caste, tradition and poverty intersect powerfully to shape prostitution. They challenge the discourse about sex work as a freely chosen occupation and point out that the vast majority of women sex workers are not accorded any dignity *as workers* and the majority of them do not opt for prostitution as free will. Global capitalist structures treat women as a commodity and that women are forced to enter into this field because they have no alternate option for survival.

Sleightholme & Sinha (1996) and Saeed (2002) also challenge the stereotype of commercial sex workers as 'bad women' and argue that information and openness about the sex industry will create an understanding of sex workers not as criminals but as victims and survivors of exploitation perpetuated by socioeconomic structures. In many cases poverty, coupled with women's insecurity and vulnerability within the family during times of crises, force them to leave their families and work as prostitutes. Despite several trafficking laws, trafficking of women is on rise because anti-trafficking interventions fail to recognise the needs of marginalised women which provide opportunities to powerful human traffickers to prey on the vulnerability of women.

In addition, Cameron & Newman (2008) note that women and girls are victimised in all regions of the world, but they are most frequently exploited in the regions where they are denied property rights, access to education, economic rights, and participation in the political processes. Therefore, trafficking in women should be seen as *a symptom of deprivation*; such deprivation acts as an important factor leading to vulnerability, and subsequently, to trafficking.

Over the last couple of decades, globalisation, with its improved efficiencies in systems of communication and transportation, and economic liberalisation has aided the emergence of a global sex industry that generates huge profits with minimum risks. Consequently, human bodies and sexualities have become products, which can be sold and purchased more easily in the global economy. As a result, the commercial exchange of sex has far exceeded its prior bounds to become a multifaceted and multi-billion dollar global industry; produced by, and, in turn, producing developments in other sectors of the global economy, for example, sex tourism, hotels, airlines (Farley 2003; Bernstein 2007; Jeffreys 2009; Shelley 2010; Kara 2011).

TRAFFICKING AND PROSTITUTION IN PAKISTAN

Prostitution is a longstanding practice, and widespread in Pakistan, especially in urban areas (Awan and Brohi 2000, Saeed 2002). It is illegal. Frequently when police recover women trafficked into prostitution, they are treated as criminals who are involved in illegal activities and consequently, are put behind the bars. Feminist research on violence against women has documented how the criminal justice system in most countries punished the victims of violence till strong movements began to change the ways in which violence has been understood and addressed within the government infrastructure. Pakistan's handling of prostitutes reflects this pattern. For example, Hussein and Hussain (2012) note that a review of some First Information Reports (FIRs) revealed that the police booked prostitutes and traffickers under the same section of the Pakistan Penal Code without further investigating whether the women were exploited by the traffickers. Therefore, many women who are trafficked into prostitution accept it as *fate accompli,* and hesitate to inform police due to fear of further victimisation and stigmatisation. This situation becomes more problematic in case of women who are internally trafficked into prostitution. Human trafficking laws in Pakistan define trafficking only in terms of crossing of international borders, so, legally, there is no trafficking within the country, and consequently, no victims of internal trafficking. In order to illustrate the disjuncture between definitions of trafficking (and prostitution) and realities on the ground, we present the voice of Amina. Amina's experiences are somewhat similar to that of Salma's since both the family members were found to be complacent in the exploitation inflicted on both women.

Amina described her experiences:

> My parents died few years ago. I have two brothers and four sisters. After the death of my parents, my two brothers forced me into prostitution. They stay at home and don't work. They force me to do all the household chores and prostitution as well. A couple of years ago, first time, I was raped by a man known to my brothers who paid them Rs 3,000 [$30]. Since then I have been continuously forced into prostitution by my brothers who keep all the money. My brothers say they don't have enough money to manage household expenditure so I have to work as prostitute. Several times, I touched their feet and begged them not to force me into prostitution. I told them that I could earn money working with my hands to financially support them, and I might work somewhere as housemaid. But, they would beat me more, even sometimes with knives. I told

> my sisters, who are all married, and some close relatives about this situation, but none of them helped me. One day, I came to know that my brothers have sold me to some person, so I ran away from home. My brothers know that I am here [in shelter]. They asked me to go back with them, but I refused them. They threatened me that once I leave the shelter, they would cut me into pieces.
>
> (a victim of trafficking, age 16 years)

Consistent with Sinha and Dasgupta's (2009) argument, there is very little 'free choice' evident in this account; however, the pattern of degradation is clear. Mostly the gender literature on violence, especially the scholarship in South Asia, frequently refers to the power of male siblings and parents (and in-laws) over young women (e.g. Kumar 1990); surprisingly, those insights are not used consistently in the international trafficking literature which remains focused within its parameters of 'public prostitution' and financial profit-making to discuss trafficking or issues of 'free choice' of prostitution as an occupation.

The gender literature offers other insights that are relevant here. As Ferree (1990) has pointed out, despite the ideologies about separate spheres of homes and public spaces and the legal edifices that claim they do not regulate what goes on within homes, in reality these spheres overlap. Thus, violence, and in Amina's case, the enforced prostitution within the home, is enabled by the lack of oversight into women's well being in the spaces where women are most vulnerable. Amina shares Salma's vulnerability as a young woman with very low status *within* her family. The cultural norms and institutionalisation of power of male relatives over *young* women centrally contribute to the situation Amina describes. Older females—Amina's sisters for instance—become complicit in the process through their silence or inaction (though we recognise they could be relatively powerless themselves).

Like Salma's case, as we present Amina's narrative, we are well aware that many people would not consider her case to be trafficking, at least, initially. The literature on trafficking assumes that women are forced into prostitution *after* they have been moved beyond their homes. Here, the woman was initiated into prostitution while she was at home, and then she was sold. If she had not run away to the shelter, she would have moved to the place designated by her buyer, and, at that time, she might have been included in the parameters of contemporary definitions of trafficking.

Yet, we would argue that this distinction does not make sense from the victim's perspective. From her standpoint, being forced into prostitution is the key issue, whether it occurs within home or outside, it is less relevant. While the causes of her immediate vulnerability—the power of her brothers—may be different from the power of traffickers and power brokers in prostitution rings or brothels according to bureaucratic definitions; according to reality, Amina has been victimised and chose to run away to avoid further oppression. Nor do the distinctions made by the Global Slavery Index about slavery, forced labour, and trafficking work well in their cases. They are bonded labourers and victims of sex trafficking.

Salma and Amina's experiences are not unique. As Jeffreys (2009) has noted, despite the fact that a significant number of women are trafficked into forced marriages, discussions on trafficking in women rarely include this dimension of trafficking. Although there are links between different forms of marriage (e.g., forced or fake marriages) and global sex commerce, marriage and trafficking are usually considered as two opposite phenomena. For example, when women are forced into marriage in return of economic or any other benefit, it becomes difficult to differentiate this from prostitution because in both the cases women and women's bodies are treated as commodities. Similarly, in many cases when women are trafficked into forced marriages, they are not treated as wives, but as domestic slaves (Shelley 2010).

This was true in Salma's case. Despite its widespread prevalence, there is lack of understanding about the nexus between marriage and trafficking in women, and as a result, the issue largely remains unaddressed. For example, in Pakistan, trafficking laws are silent about forced or fake marriages and practices such as bride price and exchange of girls and women to settle disputes. Consequently, in many cases (as noted by several victims of trafficking), traffickers use marriage as a tool to trap vulnerable girls and women, and also as a shield to escape law.

Amina and Salma's cases illustrate the point we emphasised in chapter 1: trafficking needs to be revisited as a continuum, where vulnerabilities and victimisation start well before the women are victimised in spaces away from home. From this vantage point, we reassert that trafficking has to be addressed in more nuanced ways than is in vogue now. The current discussions blurring trafficking and prostitution lead many people to equate trafficking with prostitution away from homes, which, in turn, has serious practical implications. We have already mentioned our sense of unease that trafficking for prostitution remains the principal agenda of anti-trafficking interventions (Sanghera 2005; Chew 2006; Cameron and Newman 2008). While we do not wish to minimise the gravity of this violation of human beings through commercial sex industries, we argue that anti-trafficking agenda need to be expanded.

Some scholars have pointed out that in the issue of trafficking in women, the actual problem is their powerlessness, not prostitution, and the solutions need to be focused on empowering women to counter the deceptions of traffickers who take advantage of their vulnerabilities (e.g., Brysk 2012). Also, the experiences of several countries that have adopted abolitionist or anti-abolitionist laws suggest that the menace of trafficking cannot be controlled simply through regulating prostitution; it will continue to thrive unless the issue of underlying gendered power inequalities is adequately addressed (Raymond 2002; Bernstein 2010).

Furthermore, we are also concerned about another aspect of the trafficking-as-prostitution agenda for action. Both Salma and Amina were able to go to a generic women's shelter for a period.[12] As celebrities and prominent media outlets continue to focus on sex trafficking and rescue initiatives, NGOs begin to be funded primarily for these initiatives. If, as is happening in some countries, the limited number of shelters and services in Pakistan are funded only for the 'victims of sex-trafficking' *relying on current definitions of trafficking*, then the Aminas and Salmas would remain enslaved and exploited through home-based prostitution because they would have nowhere to go.

DOES BETTER EDUCATION OR WORK EXPERIENCE PREVENT TRAFFICKING?

The sex trafficking discourse at the international level often points to education as the panacea for gendered exploitations. We also agree that education offers women new networks and expanded options in life, perhaps even work opportunities. However, we do not think access to education itself only solves the problem. Does better education alone minimise women's vulnerabilities? The following story of a trafficked woman who we refer to as Yasmin suggests that other factors might contribute to shaping the vulnerabilities of more educated women.

> I have two stepmothers. Few years back my father told me that he was no more able to financially support me, and that I had grown up and could take care of myself. I started job in an NGO. Meanwhile, I met a person who knew my family situation and asked me to marry him. I accepted his proposal, even I did not know much about him. After few days of marriage, he told me that he wanted to take me to Karachi[13] for recreation and meeting with his sister. But, after reaching

> Karachi, he sold me at a brothel in red light area. There were many girls in that brothel, majority of them had run away from their homes with their boyfriends, who later on sold them there. Some of the girls told me that before leaving their homes they were getting education in colleges/ universities. Initially when I refused to work as prostitute, owners of the brothel would beat me. But, then I accepted it as a matter of my fate because there was no way out. The girls who, with the passage of time, become addicted to that environment are really beneficial for the brothel owners, because then they don't want to go back to their homes or communities. Girls who ran away from home with their boyfriends and ended up in brothels, their parents would never accept them. In brothel, we were provided with good food and meat daily so that we remain healthy because they earn from our healthy looks and bodies. I was given Rs 500 ($5) daily. Every morning we would dress up and entertain customers till mid-night. If a girl got sick, they [brothel owners] would call a doctor there. After few months, I was able to escape and came here [shelter]. I did not contact police there because the brothel owners had contacts with them, and I had a fear that if I contacted the police, I would be put behind the bars.
>
> (a victim of trafficking, age 32 years)

In this case, unlike Amina and Salma, we get a closer look at the vulnerabilities of more educated women, some of whom had paid jobs. Yasmin worked at an NGO, but the lack of family support was a precursor to trafficking in her case. Since some of the advocacy on trafficking has repeatedly focused on traditional cultures and extremely vulnerable women (like Amina or even Salma), Yasmin's access to a more modern life reveals additional sources of vulnerabilities. In her case, marriage becomes a conduit for trafficking, as it had for other women she met in the shelter. Traffickers and pimps 'marry' women—especially women who are vulnerable because they do not have much family support—and then force them into prostitution or sell them off to brothels or individual buyers.

The other implicit pattern is equally striking: many of the women in the shelters had assumed they were participating in a modern way of life—with all the assumptions about exercising their agency and decision making power—by choosing boyfriends and partners on their own. Yet these boyfriends turned out to be traffickers who sold the women into prostitution. Traffickers and brothel owners then silenced the women through violence and threats to harm them and their families. As a result, these women cannot seek justice and protection of the law (Awan and Brohi 2000; Jalalzai 2002; Haider 2005; Amin 2010; Hussein and Hussain 2012). At the same time, there is the contradictory sense of being cared for, security in terms of food, or the visits from doctor. While the intention of the brothel owners may have been to avoid customers' perceptions about these women' ill-health—and consequent lack of desirability as sex objects—in reality, these provisions, food and occasional medical support are stark reminders about the lack of options for the women outside the brothels. Implied in this conversation is the fact that food (and medical care) is for the purpose of making them look desirable; presumably, once they grew older, and were not as attractive as sex commodities, such provisions would not be available.

The point we made earlier about generic shelters applies in Yasmin's case too. She is able to come to a shelter. However, the larger question remains: since shelters are not able to accommodate the women for the rest of their lives what is likely to happen to these women once they have to leave the shelters? Asking the question in this way leads us to the other issues we raised in chapter one: women are vulnerable to different kinds of trafficking, often repeatedly, at different points of their lives, as they move from place to place within the country or across countries.

The next case illustrates ongoing and multiple vulnerabilities of victims who cross international borders.

MULTIPLE VULNERABILITIES AND REPEATED EXPLOITATION

"Asefa" was trafficked from Afghanistan to Pakistan at the age of eight. She described her experience in the following words:

> Due to poverty and hunger, I was sold by my parents in Afghanistan for Rs 200,000 [approx. $2,000] at the age of eight years. I was bought by a family in Gujranwala [a district in Punjab, Pakistan] for domestic slavery. I was treated harshly by the family members and was frequently beaten for nothing. When I came to Pakistan, I even could not speak or understand Urdu [the local language]. After few years, I was forced by the mistress to marry her relative who was an old man [he was more than forty years age], and was already married. When I refused to marry him, I was beaten by the family. They told me that they owned me because they had purchased me from my parents. Therefore, they could do whatever they want. I was forcefully married to that old guy through fake marriage certificate without *Nikah*. My husband went abroad, and after a couple of months, I ran away from home because I was frequently abused physically and psychologically by my in-laws. When I left home, I had no idea where to go for help. I went to the office of an NGO and they suggested me to go to 'thana' [police station]. I did not know that 'thana' meant police station. When I went to the police station, I was put

> behind the bars in the ladies police station. After listening to my story, one police official advised me to say in the court that I want to go to shelter. When I was presented in the court, I said the same what the police official had told me, and the court ordered to send me here [shelter].
>
> (a foreign victim of trafficking)

Asefa's experiences fit the formal definition of a trafficked person for bonded labour. When she was a child, she was sold and forced to cross an international boundary for the purposes of providing domestic labour in conditions of servitude. Then she was forced into 'a marriage' and was physically and sexually abused. It is important to note Asefa's point about the lack of a *Nikah*. Since there is a prevailing idea among many anti-trafficking advocates that Islamic cultures treat women badly because of the tenets of Islam,[14] Asefa's point is an important corrective to that stereotype. *Nikah* ceremonies, central to Islamic principles of marriages, confirm the rights of women to freely contract a marriage. So the 'traditional' arranged marriage here violates the customary principle of Islam in order to force the young girl into a marriage with a forty-year old man.

Asefa's account shows patterns of vulnerabilities we have discussed earlier. She has little status or family support; her family sold her for profit. She was sold by her parents and bought to work in a female-type job as domestic servant, where her work conditions, and the payment of money to acquire her, positioned her as a slave in the family. In this position, she is like a 'purchased slave' as Salma described earlier. Then Asefa was forced into a polygamous marriage with an older man, and ultimately ended up in a shelter for women (after a period of imprisonment). We do not know if the family who bought her initially received money for this enforced marriage. Asefa's account that the Pakistani household told her they could do whatever they wanted because they had 'bought her' and 'owned her' would suggest they were unlikely to have simply arranged a marriage for her. If our conjecture is true, she was trafficked twice, first by her parents who profited financially, and then by the buyers who profited financially again.

Asefa has an additional problem as she did not know the local language (as she stated, she could not understand the word for a police station, the place where she thought she might get justice). Furthermore, the drawbacks of existing legislation in countries and how these are enforced become significant deterrents for Asefas of this world. Asefa was initially considered to be an illegal immigrant because she did not have 'sufficient proof' to convince people that she was a victim of trafficking. In her seminal book on Asian migrants to the United States, Espiritu (2007) discussed the effect of the gendered/raced anti-prostitution Page Laws that controlled the entry of Asian women to the US in the 19th century. Asian women had to prove they were NOT prostitutes, a near impossible task. The task of proving someone is a victim of trafficking and not a freely decided illegal immigrant is similarly daunting for women and girls like Asefa. Trafficking, under the circumstances she described, suggest there would be little paper-work available. How could she prove that she was trafficked? So a critical issue is: how should victims of trafficking be identified as different from illegal migrants through the bureaucratic process?

Once Asefa reached a shelter, the management of the shelter acted promptly and took up this case with the justice system to persuade them that the girl was being exploited, and could not be sent to prison as a criminal. While the management of the shelter was able to get Asefa some degree of protection, it is not clear, how the state would deal with her as a trafficked victim. Several organisations and practitioners report that majority of women and girls who are trafficked from other countries to Pakistan for commercial sexual exploitation are charged as criminals and sent to jails. Without any legal assistance, often these linguistically-isolated women remain in jails for long period of time, hoping for justice and support from the state. Yet, anti-trafficking advocates and scholars have documented that during this time, the traffickers, with assistance from the jail authorities, are able to contact them and further harass them (Lawyers for Human Rights and Legal Aid 1996; Awan and Brohi 2000; Munir 2003).

Many nation-states, including Pakistan, continue, in practice, to treat trafficking as a part of their traditional national-security framework. From this perspective, the state considers the phenomenon of trafficking as security threat that requires strict immigration laws and border control. This approach fails to acknowledge how both traffickers and the state itself pose threats to the security of vulnerable people who become victims of trafficking (Lobasz 2009). We will return to this issue of national security vs human security later, but the presence of thousands of refugees—from the prolonged wars in this part of the world—suggests that simply securing national borders will not solve the problem of refugees or IDPs who are vulnerable to trafficking.

LIMITATIONS OF EXISTING GENDER LITERATURE ON TRAFFICKING

Trafficking cannot be restricted primarily to the debates about criminalising prostitution or otherwise. One of the main limitations of debate on trafficking from a gender perspective has been its primary focus on prostitution rather than the multifaceted nature of trafficking (Obokata 2006). While the gender literature in general has focused on sexual exploitation to raise consciousness about this widespread social malaise, it has not successfully melded other research on gendered work and life inequities into the literature on trafficking. Thus, we find that trafficking for other purposes is largely ignored or less emphasised, for example, there are few links to forced/fake marriage, beggary, domestic servitude, or organ removal. In addition, Outshoorn (2005) notes that one of the major limitations of contextualising trafficking within prostitution frame is that it is really difficult to mark a clear boundary between forced prostitution and sex work as free choice. Although feminists have been successful in identifying prostitution as a transnational issue that needs to be addressed at global level, how to actually address the issue still remains a matter of dispute among them (Jeffreys 2003). It is important to understand that the phenomenon of trafficking is deeply intertwined in intersections of gendered/classed/raced global and local political and economic structures and power relations that create repeated cycles of vulnerability for some segments of population. The narratives of Salma, Amina and Asefa elaborate that children or young women or girls who have low levels of education, belong to low income groups, especially from rural or less developed areas or refugee camps, are more vulnerable to trafficking. Families are complicit in the process; family related common factors include family disintegration, gendered physical, sexual and psychological abuse, families in debt, and everyday gender discrimination within families (Sen and Nair 2005). The global and national level factors, especially political unrest and lack of economic options are central to the victims' narratives. The long wars and military engagements by the super-powers, and the rise of violent insurgencies and militia in the region are part of the contributory factors that lead to trafficking. Furthermore, while the United Nations expects states to combat trafficking, states like Pakistan, which spend a significant portion of their budget on security, are rarely able to address the underlying economic and social vulnerabilities that lead to trafficking. Yet, the gender literature is mostly silent on the complicity of nations, including super-powers, in facilitating such prolonged conflicts.

Another major limitation of gender literature on trafficking is that it focuses overwhelmingly on women only. The underlying assumption is that because of power imbalances between men and women, only women are vulnerable to trafficking. In reality, trafficking is a manifestation of vulnerabilities of both men and women. Human trafficking, as Shelley (2010) notes, is a crime in which women are significantly represented not only as victims, but also as perpetrators who facilitate exploitation of other women, and activists as well seeking to fight trafficking. In many cases, women are major actors involved in exploitation of other women (e.g., in domestic servitude and running brothels).

Likewise, Connell (2005) argues that owing to the assumption that gender issue is only relevant to women, efforts to incorporate gender perspective in policies focus on addressing the concerns of women only. As a result, issues and concerns of men are mostly left ignored. Although men generally gain from patriarchal gender order, not all men get in the same way because patriarchal gender order is intervened with other hierarchal relations (e.g., class, race, ethnicity, nationality). Therefore, Connell notes that analysing gendered structures should not only reveal a pattern of advantages for men, but also a linked pattern of disadvantages. Men, for instance, collectively gain more through the gender division of labour for they receive more resources and take up most of the managerial positions. At the same time, some men are disadvantaged for being engaged in hazardous occupations and suffer from occupational injuries. In addition, men experience heavier social pressure to remain employed to fulfil the role of breadwinner for their families. The men who benefit from this gender division of labour have different life experiences than the men who are disadvantaged. Therefore, the men who are disadvantaged may share more common experiences and interests with the women in their communities than with the other (advantaged) men.

TRAFFICKING IN MEN

Moving away almost from the exclusive focus on trafficking for sexual exploitation, in this section, we draw attention to the trafficking in men. While a great deal of trafficking literature ignores the vulnerability of men, it implicitly or otherwise reinforces men's dominance over women. Usually counter-trafficking interventions consider only women vulnerable to exploitation, assuming men as perpetrators of abuse. This assumption not only ignores the vulnerabilities of particular men, but also reinforces men's dominance over women who need to be 'saved' from (bad) men by (good) men. Due to dearth of information and underreporting of trafficking in men, the issue still remains an invisible dimension of trafficking (Skeldon 2000; Ditmore 2005; Rosenberg 2010).

Trafficking of men can certainly include trafficking for the purposes of sexual exploitation. In this section, we focus on two other types of exploitation that are the objects of trafficking. Interviews with the men who were victims of trafficking for forced/bonded labour and organ removal reveal several dimensions of vulnerabilities associated with 'masculinity'. Owing to strong prevailing patriarchal norms, especially in rural area, Pakistani men tend to be the sole breadwinners for their families. However, the high level of poverty, rising inflation and diminishing livelihood opportunities have severely altered the societal position of men. As a result, men are susceptible to be trafficked into debt bondage or forced labour.

In poverty stricken areas, moneylenders (usually local landlords and brick kiln owners) provide small-scale loans to the poor people who are uneducated, devoid of skills, and do not have any economic asset or security deposit to borrow credit from the organised sectors. Men usually take loans when someone in family falls ill or dies, or in order to pay for the weddings of their daughters and sisters. Well aware of the needs and vulnerabilities of these poor people, traffickers exploit these opportunities to trap such men/families in a never-ending cycle of exploitation. In the absence of availability of any social safety nets, many men approach local landlords for small loans, usually ranging between Rs 30,000 and 50,000 ($300-$500). After getting loan, these persons and their families are bound to work in brick kilns or on agriculture lands owned by the moneylenders, and/or they work as domestic servants in the homes of moneylenders. Although the families—men, women and children—work daily for long hours (usually 14-16 hours), the families earn daily wages between Rs 700 and 1000 ($7-$10) only. Of this meagre amount of money, the moneylenders deduct fifty per cent as payment towards the outstanding loan. This means that many families are never able to repay the loan because the wage they receive in return of their labour is hardly enough to feed the family. Meanwhile, as the poor people are unable to save anything, they take loans repeatedly during family crises, and thus, the debt increases. Being trapped in a vicious circle of exploitation, children provide family labour in these brick kilns or agricultural lands. ILO's Forced Labour Reports (2013, 2014) document some of these work conditions and efforts to address them. Some children are also subject to domestic servitude at the homes of moneylenders. As these children do not find any opportunity to get an education or acquire some skill to earn better futures, they remain trapped in poverty and vicious circle of exploitation like their parents. Many parents do wish to send their children to schools, but education is secondary priority when it comes to the question of basic survival. As one of the interviewees, who was a victim of debt bondage, said "We do want our children to get education and leave this area. But, when we don't have enough food to feed them even for two times a day, how can you think we should send them to schools?"

Enslavement in this form of labour sets the men and women up for another form of trafficking that has not been elaborately discussed in the literature: organ trafficking. Arguably organ trafficking is not exactly the same as trafficking for labour (and/or sexual exploitation). But, if we rethink of sex trafficking which is not just the use of human body, but the sexual use of woman's body, wherein her humanness is reduced only to specific body parts, including vagina, anus, breast and mouth (Veen 2001; Farley 2003), then we can see a link to organ trafficking. The rapid growth of the organ market, the targeting of poor men and women who are often reeling under the systems of bonded labour, and the transfer of these 'commodities' for clandestine profit, position this process well within the ambit of trafficking. It certainly highlights the repeated cycles of exploitation which are embedded within trafficking.

'Abbas' said:

> I sold my kidney because I had to pay a loan of Rs 150,000 [$1,500] to the brick kiln owner. Although my whole family was working in the brick kiln, the amount of loan was increasing with the passage of time. I had to take loan repeatedly for the treatment of my mother, then my son fell ill, and I had to marry [off] my daughter. After working the whole day, we earn only Rs 400-500 [$4-$5], whereas just to feed the whole family we need Rs 600 [$6] daily. What else can we do to survive if don't take loans?
>
> (a victim of debt bondage/organ removal, age 35 years)

Until the debt is paid, the family cannot leave the area, and they remain as virtual property of the moneylender. In this situation of extreme power imbalance, in some cases, girls and women are also sexually abused by the moneylenders. This cycle of exploitation continues as the family never finds enough means to repay the loan, and the debt is passed on from husband to wife, father to son, through the generations (Bales 2005). Although many people would believe that hereditary slavery was abolished when slavery was outlawed, it is a bitter reality that even today some people are still born into hereditary slavery, for example, in case of debt bondage (Global Slavery Index 2013).

'Rahman' describes why he sold his kidney:

> I inherited a loan of Rs 200,000 [$2,000] from my father. My elder daughter works as domestic servant in the home of the moneylender, whereas rest of the family works in the brick kiln. I and my other family members were frequently physically abused by the landlord. I could not bear this humiliation of my family and decided to sell my kidney for Rs 175,000 [$1,750]. I hope I will be able to return the remaining amount soon.
>
> (a victim of debt bondage/organ removal, age 30 years)

As the victims of debt bondage like Abbas or Rahman tend to be illiterate, they hardly understand the terms of their loan and completely depend on the moneylenders regarding calculations of their outstanding debt, which further enhance the coercive power of the moneylenders and ensure their continued servitude (UNDP 2007). Moreover, the TIP Report (2013) notes that some feudal landlords, who are involved in debt bondage, have political affiliation or links with authorities and use their social, economic, and political influence to exploit poor people. Even in some cases when bonded labourers approach police to flee from the violence of landlords, the police, instead of protecting them, return them to the landlords who then hold them and their families in private jails. This certainly discourages other bonded labourers to seek help from the police.

Taking advantage of vulnerable positions of the families, organ traffickers approach them through agents or body brokers and give them false hopes that the only way they can get rid of their loan and atrocities of the moneylenders is to sell kidney. Although both men and women become victims of organ trafficking, according to a body broker who was interviewed for this study, men by large outnumber women because they are mainly responsible to arrange money during times of family crises. Moreover, in many cases, to protect their honour, men sell kidneys because they cannot see or bear the moneylenders abusing the women physically, psychologically and sexually. This is a different form of honour maintenance—diametrically opposite to honour killings which regularly make global news. In addition, in the conservative Muslim society, many men do not think it morally appropriate to let the male doctors see the naked bodies of their wives/daughters.

'Usman' said:

> We sell our body to protect honour of our women. We cannot see or bear our women sexually abused by the landlords. We do it because we are helpless and do not have any other option. Allowing others [doctors] to see naked bodies is a matter of shame and dishonour. We can show our bodies, but cannot allow others to see naked bodies of our women.
>
> (a victim of debt bondage/organ removal, age 28 years)

On an average, a person receives approximately Rs 175,000 [$1,750] for selling his/her kidney, whereas an agent or broker, who plays the role of middleman, receives Rs 15,000 [$150] as commission from the victim of organ trafficking. People sell their body parts with the hope that they will get rid of loan and come out of the cycle of exploitation. But, unfortunately, most of them are unable to break the vicious circle of exploitation even after selling their body parts. Our data indicate that many victims of organ trade/debt bondage were initially able to repay the loan, but soon they were again trapped into a new cycle of exploitation because they could not find any alternate source of livelihood. Consequently, they again approached the moneylenders for loans in order to feed their families.

Moreover, these victims of organ trade said that *after* the removal of kidney, they were not able to perform hard labour or lift heavy weights. Thus, they were deprived of their only economic asset (i.e., labour). Consequently, their capacity to earn wages dropped significantly, and they were again forced to take loans from the moneylenders generating new cycles of vulnerability and exploitation.

Although the UN protocol on trafficking clearly defines exploitation of human beings for the purpose of organ removal as a form of trafficking, neither the scholarly literature on trafficking nor the counter-trafficking laws in Pakistan consider organ trade as a form of trafficking. Due to the lack of legislation regarding organ trade and transplantation, Pakistan was considered as one of the leading countries in terms of 'transplant tourism' and organ trade, where thousands of illegal transplants were performed each year (Pearson 2004; Shah 2004; Naqvi *et al.* 2007; Shimazono 2007). Owing to the interventions of the Supreme Court of Pakistan which took notice of the growing numbers of organ trade in the country and directed the government to regulate organ transplantation, the federal government promulgated the Transplantation of Human Organs and Tissues Act (2009) in March 2010. It is believed that cases of organ trade have been reduced after passing the new law which prohibits the trade of human organs and prescribes strict punishments for those who are found to be involved in illegal transplantation or sale or purchase of organs (Kazim 2008; Bile *et al.* 2010).

INTERLOCKING SYSTEMS OF EXPLOITATION

In this chapter we examined trafficking through a gender lens. Consistent with the data that indicate large number of women are trafficked for sexual exploitation, we began the discussion with a focus on sex trafficking. Consistent with other studies, we found that patriarchy intersects with poverty to create conditions rife for trafficking. However, parting ways with the dominant focus of discussion—whether prostitution is the main objective of trafficking (and its ancillary discussion about the role of agency and choice in the process), we emphasised the multiple forms of exploitation that victims often face. We also pointed out that political instability along with economic and social volatility foster conditions for trafficking.

Following our discussion on women, we moved onto the trafficking of men. Here again, it was apparent that the gendered nature of trafficking sorts men vs women for different types of labour, though neither group is completely immune from sexual exploitation or labour bondage. We further focused on a relatively new recognition of organ trafficking as part of the larger discussion. This too is a classed/gendered process. More importantly, people are exploited differently at different stages of their experience as trafficked victims. Persons who become victims of trafficking also experience other forms of violence and exploitation which are interconnected with each other. For example, this research shows that people who became victims of forced labour or debt bondage had experienced political and economic structural violence which made them vulnerable to trafficking. Being trafficked into debt bondage, their vulnerabilities were further enhanced, which were subsequently abused by the organ traffickers. Even after their repeated exploitation, the victims of trafficking were not able to break the vicious circles of vulnerability and exploitation. Therefore, the complex nature of trafficking can be better understood by situating it within interlocking systems of exploitation as one cycle of exploitation leads to or causes the generation of other cycles of vulnerability and exploitation. As a result of these multiple causes and cycles of vulnerability, trafficking cannot be addressed as one time phenomenon through any short term humanitarian or rescue approach.

CHAPTER 4
Human Trafficking: A Human Rights Paradigm

> Violations of human rights are both a cause and a consequence of trafficking in persons. Accordingly, it is essential to place the protection of all human rights at the centre of any measures taken to prevent and end trafficking. Anti-trafficking measures should not adversely affect the human rights and dignity of persons and, in particular, the rights of those who have been trafficked, migrants, internally displaced persons, refugees and asylum-seekers. (UNHCHR 2002:3)

According to Sen (1998:40), "the notion of human rights builds on the idea of a shared humanity". In this sense, human rights are the rights one acquires by birth since one is a human being, and therefore, they are held universally by all human beings (Donnelly 2007; Osiaty'nski 2009). The Universal Declaration of Human Rights (UDHR)—considered as the founding document of modern human rights, and accepted by all countries—affirms the inherent human dignity and worth of every person in the world, without any distinction.[15] According to Article 2 of the UDHR, "Everyone is entitled to all the rights and freedoms set forth in this Declaration, without distinction of any kind, such as race, colour, sex, language, religion, political or other opinion, national or social origin, property, birth or other status. Furthermore, no distinction shall be made on the basis of the political, jurisdictional or international status of the country or territory to which a person belongs, whether it be independent, trust, non-self-governing or under any other limitation of sovereignty". Further, Article 4 of the Convention proclaims, "No one shall be held in slavery or servitude; slavery and the slave trade shall be prohibited in all their forms". Likewise, Article 8 of the International Covenant on Civil and Political Rights (1966), and Articles 6 and 7 of the International Covenant on Economic, Social and Cultural Rights (1966) clearly state that no human being shall be held in slavery or forced labour, and everyone has the right to favourable working conditions and decent living.

Thus, theoretically, a trafficked person should have rights laid down in the UDHR and other human rights instruments, including rights to legal recourse. The reality is, however, far more complicated.

Trafficking in human beings, the fastest growing criminal industry in the world is a gross violation of human dignity and human rights. All individuals who are subject to trafficking are denied the fundamental right to freedom. Analysing trafficking as a process that starts from the recruitment of vulnerable people leading to their exploitation shows the violation of human rights at every step of trafficking. Trafficking involves violation of several human rights, including political-civil-economic-social-cultural rights. For example, if we think about the narratives of Salma, Amina, Yasmin, Asefa, Abbas, Rahman and Usman, it is clear that trafficking violates political and civil rights, including the inherent right to life, the right to take part in the conduct of public affairs, the right to have equal access to public service, the right to marry with consent, the right to personal liberty and human security, the right to bodily integrity, the right to freedom of association, movement and expression, the right to freedom from torture or other cruel or inhuman treatment, the right to freedom from discrimination, and the right to freedom from compulsory labour and servitude in all their forms. Trafficking also violates social-cultural-economic rights, for example, the right to health, education and adequate standard of living, the right to fair wages and equal remuneration for equal work without any discrimination and the right to safe and healthy working conditions (Kostanyan 2012). Most commonly, people who become victims of trafficking are those who are deprived politically, socially, and economically. They lack power to escape or challenge the trappings of powerful traffickers who use various methods to condition their victims, including starvation, confinement and physical, sexual, psychological abuse and threats of violence to victims and their families (Birkenthal 2011; Mills 2011).

As we documented in the last chapter, trafficking reflects significant violations of a person's human dignity and the rights he/she is supposed to enjoy against exploitation. A merger of human rights and gender approaches offers a more productive frame through which we can consider trafficking. According to Pearce (2011), the employment of a human rights framework appears to be the best strategy to close disparities of power and resources, and to develop new codes to alter human relationships that would ultimately address the deep causes of human vulnerability and insecurity.

With reference to trafficking in human beings, Obokata (2006) argues that there are two dimensions of human rights framework: framework of analysis and framework of action. As a framework of analysis applying a human rights framework helps identifying relevant human rights principles in relation to trafficking (e.g., right to life, health, prohibition of torture and slavery). As a framework of action, it urges states to take practical steps to counter trafficking, prosecute traffickers and protect the rights of their citizens. A human rights framework, therefore, can be more effective in terms of making states accountable to address the human rights issues involved in the process of trafficking.

Moreover, Brysk and Choi-Fitzpatrick (2012) note that situating trafficking within the human rights paradigm helps to shape responses to trafficking not as a moral problem or of cultural backwardness, but as an issue of violations of human rights that make people vulnerable to exploitation. The argument is that counter-trafficking interventions need to be based on international human rights norms with focus on protecting and restoring rights by way of ensuring human security overall, even if it does not fit within the ambit of state security and the need of states to secure its borders.

As we described in the last chapter, the prevalence of discriminatory practices and gender-based violence continue to play a significant role in making women and children more vulnerable to trafficking. According to Article 6 of the Convention on the Elimination of All Forms of Discrimination Against Women (CEDAW), "State Parties shall take all appropriate measures, including legislation, to suppress all forms of traffic in women and exploitation of prostitution of women". Some common forms of violence that contribute significantly to the trafficking in women include the violation of reproductive rights, domestic violence, violence perpetrated through public policies, and the violation of women's rights to decision making, especially pertaining to access and control over resources (Sen and Nair 2005).

All the cases we discussed in the last chapter involved some form of extreme coercion, violence and abuse. From that perspective, they all exemplify gender-based violence. Even trafficking in men's organs involves bonded labour, coercion and the construction of vulnerabilities among poor men. Gender-based violence is a violation of human rights and to highlight violations of women's rights across the world, the statement "women's rights are human rights" was included in the Beijing Declaration at the end of the Fourth World Conference on Women in 1995 (Gaer 2001; Merry 2006). Despite several international instruments and conventions on women's human rights, gender-based violence is widespread and still remains a global challenge because it is usually perceived as an individual's deviant act or cultural practice of 'others' without realising it a phenomenon that is deeply embedded in global political and economic structures (Dauer 2001; Gaer 2001; Merry 2006; Erturk and Purkayastha 2012).

Trafficking further highlights the effects of structural inequalities and macro and micro level violence on the vulnerabilities of victims. Though this literature focuses primarily on women, if we used an intersectional approach for understanding human rights—which is its intent—then the vulnerabilities of men to violence and trafficking would become a more prominent part of the conversation.

Further elaborating the links between gender, human rights and trafficking, Sen and Nair (2005) argue that the concept of gender mainstreaming in the human rights paradigm stresses the equal enjoyment of human rights by women and men. Development approaches based on a human rights and gender-responsive framework help reduce power inequalities and ensure well-being and empowerment of both men and women. Accordingly, a human rights approach to counter trafficking should be gender-responsive to address the issue of resource disparities and power inequalities between men and women to prevent violations of their human rights.

HUMAN RIGHTS AND ANTI-TRAFFICKING INTERVENTIONS

While developing anti-trafficking laws and interventions, the UN urges states to emphasise the primacy of human rights. For example, the UN Recommended Principles and Guidelines on Human Rights and Human Trafficking recommend:

1. The human rights of trafficked persons shall be at the centre of all efforts to prevent and combat trafficking, and to protect, assist and provide redress to victims.
2. States have a responsibility under international law to act with due diligence to prevent trafficking to investigate and prosecute traffickers and to assist and protect trafficked persons. (UNHCHR 2002:3)

Although the Recommended Principles provide a broader framework to contextualise and address trafficking as a human rights issue, the guidelines are designed mainly viewing trafficking as an issue of migration. At this level, Asefa's case would be addressed as part of due diligence to prosecute traffickers and protect trafficked persons. The guidelines, however, provide little help in terms of dealing with the issue of internal trafficking; Salma, Amina and Yasmin would not be helped, nor would Rahman, Abbas or Usman.

Despite the UN guidelines to frame human rights-based response to trafficking, there has been a common tendency among law enforcement agencies across the countries of viewing trafficking only as an issue of illegal migration or crime against the state. As a result, the common response of governments has been to deport trafficked persons without understanding that *trafficking is primarily a crime against the individual whose rights have been violated* initially by traffickers and later on by the state through forced deportation (Aronowitz 2002; Segrave *et al.* 2009). Moreover, due to certain presumptions about trafficking, support to a victim of trafficking is dependent on his/her telling the story that should fit into the predefined essentialist nature of deserving victim. For example, deserving victims of trafficking are assumed to be women and children—forced into commercial sexual exploitation—who have been trafficked from uncivilised societies due to their cultural backwardness and need to be rescued by law enforcement agencies. More importantly, as Grant (2014) argued, focusing on brothels and rescues, such as the action of individuals who "buy" girls from brothels to "free" them, make for good news; but these actions are too limited to really address the causes of vulnerabilities. Nor do the rescue initiatives ensure these victims can access the entire gamut of their human rights and experience human security, i.e. build lives of dignity based on their ability to substantively access all human rights.

Usually counter-trafficking interventions are based on the dichotomous category of "victim or criminal", in which support is provided to only those who are considered as deserving victims, whereas others who do not fit into the predefined category of deserving victims are treated as criminals (Jordan 2002; Hua and Nigorizawa 2010). If we take the case of Asefa, whether she is a victim or a criminal depends as to where these terms are being defined. Unless there is a convergence of these varying meanings of terms to promote action, it is not always clear that Asefa will emerge as a victim. Consequently, anti-trafficking interventions tend to further victimise trafficked persons, including men, women and children. Despite the fact that the Recommended Principles and Guidelines on Human Rights and Human Trafficking (UNHCHR 2002:3) emphasise that "States shall ensure that trafficked persons are protected from further exploitation and harm and have access to adequate physical and psychological care. Such protection and care shall not be made conditional upon the capacity or willingness of the trafficked person to cooperate in legal proceedings"; generally only those victims of trafficking are provided support who agree to cooperate with law enforcement agencies in prosecution of the traffickers (Chapkis 2003; Hua and Nigorizawa 2010). Several studies show that many victims of trafficking who are deported immediately after 'rescuing' again fall prey to traffickers (Konrad 2008).

Furthermore, it is not sufficient to focus mostly on political and civil rights of the victims. Social rights to work (for fair wages), education and health are central to anti-trafficking efforts. If we reflect on each of the cases as we presented in the last chapter, the victims are young females or males, they had to be somewhat healthy to be able to work or sell their kidneys. For both the men and women then, what is being sold is related to their health. For the organ-seller, his/her health is not supposed to be the commercial commodity for sale. Yet, that is what happens: the men fall into longer cycles of ill-health and are unable to work or pay off their debts. In the case of the women in the commercial sex industry, there is some attention to their health since the market demands healthy women for sex. However, as we mentioned, this attention to their health is age delimited, once they are older and no longer profitable commodities, inevitably their health is negatively affected.

LIMITATIONS OF HUMAN RIGHTS FRAMEWORK

Some scholars (e.g., Jordan 2001; Abu-Lughod 2002; Bales 2005; Kempadoo 2005; Merry 2006; Holmes 2010; Hua 2011) also highlight some limitations of human rights framework and note that the tendency to universalise human rights sometimes reinforces agenda of the Western societies. They challenge the globally dominant discourse on human trafficking developed in the West and argue that existing conceptualisation of trafficking ignores the ground realities in the global South because root causes of trafficking are embedded in the global hegemonic structures of inequality. People in the global South are generally considered vulnerable to trafficking because of their repressive cultures and failure on part of the governments to protect the people without realising how global political-economic systems are affecting the capacity of states in the global South to protect their citizens from exploitation. Multinational corporations and global financial institutions wield more power and resources than many so-called sovereign nation states in the global South; these global institutions dictate the states' domestic policies. In reality, these policies—usually carried out in the name of structural adjustment programmes—sanction capitalist free markets and have had produced devastating effects on the lives of poor people in the global South (Mutua 2008; Gibney and Skogly 2010; Armaline, Glasberg and Purkayastha 2011).

Accordingly, the rescue approach fails to address the root causes of trafficking deeply intertwined in intersections of global and local political-economic structures and power relations that create repeated cycles of vulnerability for some segments of population. As we have discussed earlier, trafficking occurs within a continuum and interlocking systems of violence. Therefore, it cannot be addressed simply through rescuing trafficked persons without targeting factors that perpetuate those cycles of vulnerability.

Moreover, with reference to the rescue model, it also becomes important to analyse the role of NGOs, both international and local, in addressing the menace of trafficking. According to some scholars (e.g., Bulbeck 1998; Bukovska 2008; Mutua 2008; Chowdhury 2011), many international human rights NGOs and donor agencies—usually supported by the West—claim to protect marginalised people in the global South, but themselves are involved in corrupt practices and exploit poor people, especially women, for their own benefits. The NGOs promote the agenda of their donors, and do not always address the structural inequalities. Moreover, the efforts of many local grass-root level organisations which are involved in activism and fight for the rights of the marginalised people are rarely acknowledged or supported by the international organisations. Thus, the Western-led humanitarian interventions in the global South usually treat victims only as passive objects who need outside protection and reinforce the ongoing efforts to control the savage of the uncivilised by the civilised West (Chowdhury 2011).

Likewise, while highlighting the NGO-ification of the anti-trafficking movement in the United States, Musto (2010) argues that the current movement has severely affected the efforts of trafficked persons to organise a movement based on their experiences and needs. As the government's anti-trafficking efforts are more focused on prosecution, mainly NGOs have become responsible to provide services for the protection to the trafficked persons. NGOs that receive anti-trafficking funds from the governments must follow the government's anti-prostitution policies while providing services to the trafficked persons. As a result, the NGOs are required to oppose all forms of sex work which restricts their ability to provide services to those clients or trafficked persons who have worked, forcibly or voluntarily, in the sex trade industry. In addition,

NGOs receiving funding from the government cannot challenge or speak against the government defined policies and agenda; therefore, they fail to echo the voices of trafficked persons.

In a similar vein, Bales (2005) notes that many NGOs tend to provide exaggerated statistics about prevalence of human trafficking in order to receive funding from donor agencies. Women and children, deemed as 'innocent victims', are the common humanitarian objects of protection and rescue (Brysk 2009). Although the humanitarian framework may be useful to arouse empathy and generate funding for anti-trafficking efforts, its dominant focus on rescuing innocent victims, without addressing the structural factors that perpetuate gender-based inequalities and violence, do little to combat trafficking (Mutua 2008; Crawford 2010). However, depending on the definitions and explanations of trafficking they use, the role of the international organisations may vary. In order to address the issue of power inequalities, Chowdhury (2011) asserts, reliance on the Western aid or imported individualistic welfarist model is not a solution. Creating independent and sustainable local movements, based on the existing ground realities and lived experiences of survivors of violence, can better help to bring the desired social change.

TRAFFICKING AND HUMAN RIGHTS: SITUATION IN PAKISTAN

The Constitution of the Islamic Republic of Pakistan, the premier source of legislation, requires the state to take necessary steps to protect its citizens from exploitation. For example, Article 3 of the Constitution calls upon the state to eliminate all forms of exploitation. Article 11 prohibits all forms of forced labour and trafficking in human beings whereas Articles 25(3) and 26(2) require the state to make special provision for the protection of women and children.[16] The Government of Pakistan promulgated the Prevention and Control of Human Trafficking Ordinance in 2002 to specifically address the issue of human trafficking in Pakistan.

In Pakistan—like many other countries of the world—the phenomenon of trafficking is generally perceived only as an issue of national security rather than human security. The main leading agency that has been responsible in developing and implementing the trafficking legislation is the Federal Investigation Agency (FIA) which works under the administrative control of the Ministry of Interior. While noting the general tendency among countries to organise their counter-trafficking interventions based on the assumptions of trafficking as a crime against national security, national sovereignty and border control, many scholars (e.g., Aradau 2008; Konrad 2008; Brysk 2009) argue that efforts to combat trafficking are required to implement more strict migration policies and border control. Such response further enhances the risk of victims of trafficking to be treated as illegal immigrants posing threats to national security. Conversely, situating trafficking within human security framework provides an alternate path to address trafficking as an issue of governance failure which calls for global cooperation to protect people from vulnerabilities that result from the failure of global political and economic systems (Brysk 2009). Discussions on human trafficking, however, rarely focus on the issue of human security and protection. Therefore, confusion still remains as to who deserves to be protected (Aradau 2008).

No doubt, it is the main responsibility of the government to protect the rights of citizens guaranteed by the Constitution and several human rights instruments. Anti-trafficking activities in Pakistan have, however, been mainly initiated or supported by donor agencies and NGOs. One of the main problems of NGOs taking the lead to protect people from the failure of governance is that governments shift their responsibilities on NGOs (Lekorwe and Mpabanga 2007). Given that NGOs' interventions tend to be dependent on funding from donor agencies, one of the major issues involved in their projects is sustainability since many times donor-led interventions lack a clear exit plan. Nor are donor agencies always able to sustain their support. Responding to their local politics, their funding emphasis often gets diverted. For example, a model shelter for victims of trafficking was established in Pakistan by the International Organization for Migration (IOM) with the support of a donor agency, but the project could not be sustained once the donor funding was stopped. This translates to women like Salma or Amina or Asefa finding them with no refuge once the funding disappeared. According to some stakeholders, the main reasons that the project could not continue include: prime focus of the government on combating terrorism and extremism, so the government could not provide bridge or long term funding; lack of financial resources from the government or elsewhere in the country; and, the lack of commitment and reluctance on part of the government to accept that trafficking is 'our problem'.

In Pakistan, like many other countries, victims of trafficking are identified almost exclusively by the law enforcement agencies which are usually not well trained in dealing with victims of trafficking, and tend to confuse trafficking with smuggling and illegal migration (Hussein and Hussain 2012). Thus, it depends on the judgment of the officials whether a person is recognised as a victim of trafficking or criminal. Due to lack of capacity and lacunas in existing trafficking laws, many victims of trafficking are penalised as criminals. In addition, assumptions about the gendered nature of trafficking also influence the identification of 'deserving' victim of trafficking. For example, men are assumed to be economic migrants who are involved in illegal migration, whereas women and children are considered vulnerable to trafficking (Ditmore 2005). Consequently, men are treated as criminals and interrogated in the detention centres, whereas, the women who are identified as victims of trafficking are sent to shelters.

Data from stakeholders reveal other problems with putting the criminal justice system in charge of addressing trafficking; instead, this approach may have some serious implications (Konrad 2008). Generally, police treat the statement of a victim of trafficking given soon after recovery as true and final.

However, experiences of service providers suggest that victims need some time to recover from the trauma they have experienced in order to share their stories of exploitation with anybody. The issue becomes more problematic in case of foreign victims of trafficking or women who are trafficked into prostitution. Foreign victims of trafficking, who may not speak or understand the language, require more time in developing trust in foreign authorities and institutions. Likewise, women who are trafficked into prostitution hesitate to share their experiences because of shame and the fear of stigmatisation. After recovering from trauma and developing some confidence in service providers, the victims of trafficking, however, tend to change their initial statement which is often considered suspicious by the police who treat it as victims' tactics to hide the truth or to support traffickers. Moreover, some persons subject to trafficking do not see themselves as victims of exploitation. Many victims of bonded labour/kidney trade and sexual exploitation consider their exploitation as a matter of fate; even some of them describe exploiters (e.g., moneylender, organ broker) as benevolent persons who helped them in crises. Therefore, identifying victims of trafficking or traffickers is a complex and time-consuming process which is unlikely to yield good documentation through the initial statement of the victim only (Brown 2000).

It is important to understand that the issue of human trafficking cannot be addressed through one time or short-term approaches based on humanitarian interventions or rescue model. It is the basic responsibility of every state to take necessary steps to protect the rights of its citizens, and from the human security framework grounded in human rights, to make sure citizens of other states are not harmed either. Considering human trafficking as a cause and consequence of human rights violations requires the shift of response from rescuing people to empowering them to resist and challenge the trappings of traffickers (Huda 2006). It is clear that a human rights-based response to trafficking, grounded in an understanding of gendered (intersectional) inequalities, can help direct attention to the root causes of trafficking emanating from the violations of human rights, and understanding trafficked persons as active agents—rather than passive objects—who are capable of resuming control of their lives (Jordan 2002; Crawford 2010). Unless anti-trafficking interventions are based on international human rights standards, many trafficked persons will continue to suffer serious human rights violations initially at the hands of traffickers, and subsequently, by law enforcement agencies which treat them as criminals rather than as victims of violations of human rights.

CHAPTER 5

Conceptualising Human Trafficking: Challenges and Implications

> They would not call it slavery, but some other name. Slavery has been fruitful in giving itself names . . . It has been called by a great many names, and it will call itself by yet another name; and you and I and all of us had better wait and see what new form this old monster will assume, in what new skin this old snake will come forth next.
>
> (Frederick Douglass, cited in Foner and Taylor 1999: 579)

In this chapter, we present some institutional definitions of trafficking and then discuss their limitations with reference to the theoretical arguments on the subject. Despite various treaties and conventions on human trafficking, still widespread prevalence of the phenomenon has made it a global challenging issue.

CONCEPTUALISATION OF TRAFFICKING IN HISTORICAL PERSPECTIVE

The initial understanding of trafficking, during the early 20th century, was based on the assumption that trafficking was conducted for "immoral purposes", defined as prostitution or sexual exploitation of women, rather than the exploitation of human beings (Sietske 1995). This assumption was reflected in several international instruments on human trafficking adopted during the 20th century. Obokata (2006) and Segrave *et al.* (2009) provide a brief background of international instruments on human trafficking, assumptions about trafficking which guided these instruments, and their limitations. The first international instrument to counter trafficking was the International Agreement for the Suppression of the White Slave Trade (1904),[17] signed on 18 May 1904, and entered into force on 18 July 1905. The Agreement defined trafficking as the compulsive procuring of women or girls abroad for immoral purposes. The hallmark of this particular time period was economic stagnant conditions in Europe which were believed to be a key factor in selling women and girls for prostitution. According to Article 1 of the Agreement, "Each of the Contracting Governments undertakes to establish or name some authority charged with the coordination of all information relative to the procuring of women or girls for immoral purposes abroad; this authority shall be empowered to correspond direct with the similar department established in each of the other Contracting States". Further, "immoral purposes" were explained in Article 3 that proclaimed:

> The Governments undertake, when the case arises, and within legal limits, to have the declarations taken of women or girls of foreign nationality who are prostitutes, in order to establish their identity and civil status, and to discover who has caused them to leave their country. The information obtained shall be communicated to the authorities of the country of origin of the said women and girls, with a view to their eventual repatriation.

Some of the main limitations of this Agreement included: trafficking was reduced only to the procurement of girls and women abroad for prostitution; assumptions about gender and race played a significant role in defining trafficking because it was limited to white women only; and, the Agreement did not mention any preventive measures on part of the contracting states to control trafficking. Later on, in 1910, the International Convention for the Suppression of the White Slave Traffic[18] revised the earlier definition of trafficking and included coercion or deception as important elements of trafficking in women and girls (more than twenty years of age). The Convention was still limited to the white slave traffic only and did not include women in brothels under the definition of trafficking leaving it up to the states to deal with women in brothels according to their own domestic legislations. The significant feature of this Convention was to make the contracting parties responsible to take action against those who were involved in the white slave trade and required them to amend their national laws accordingly.

After the World War I, under the auspices of the League of Nations, two more international instruments on trafficking were adopted: first in 1921 and second in 1933. The first instrument, the International Convention for the Suppression of the Traffic in Women and Children (1921),[19] was built on the recommendations contained in the Final Act of the International Conference summoned by the Council of the League of Nations between 30th June and 5th July 1921. Article 2 of the Convention (1921) first time recognised the trafficking in children of both sexes and required the contracting parties to prosecute those who were found involved in the trafficking of children of both sexes. Moreover, Article 5 increased the age limit for protection from twenty to twenty one completed years. Compared with the previous international agreements on trafficking, this Convention (1921) was especially significant in terms of recognising trafficking in women for all because it did not limit trafficking to white women only. Subsequently, the second international agreement at the behest of the League of Nations was the International Convention for the Suppression of the Traffic in Women of Full Age(1933).[20] According to Article 1 of the Convention (1933), "Whoever, in order to gratify the passions of another person, has procured, enticed or led away even with her consent, a woman and girl of full age for immoral purposes to be carried out in another country, shall be punished, notwithstanding that the various acts constituting the offence may have been committed in different countries". Thus, the Convention (1933) defined consent of women as irrelevant in the process of trafficking, whereas in the earlier agreements the issue of consent was considered irrelevant only in case of children. Due to the narrow focus of the aforementioned international instruments on trafficking, they failed to adequately address the issue of trafficking. Consequently, it led to the adoption of another international agreement—the first under the auspices of the UN—the Convention for the Suppression of the Traffic in Persons and of the Exploitation of the Prostitution of Others (1949).[21] Like previous instruments, this Convention (1949) reduced trafficking to prostitution only. However, it adopted a gender-neutral language and used word 'person' instead of 'women' signifying that men could also be trafficked for sexual exploitation. In addition, the Convention (1949) defined trafficking in terms of both within and across states. As the Convention (1949) equated trafficking with prostitution, the contracting states were required to take necessary action to abolish brothels and punish those who managed or financed brothels.

Furthermore, Obokata (2006) notes that though trafficking has its roots in slavery and the slave trade of Africans, the international community has considered trafficking—owing to its association with prostitution—morally distinct from slavery. As a result, more interest and efforts were invested in dealing with the issue of trafficking than the slave trade which is why during the period of early 20th century to the mid-20th century five international instruments on trafficking were adopted, while only two were on slavery (1926 and 1956).

CONTEMPORARY CONCEPTUALISATION OF HUMAN TRAFFICKING

Despite having so many international instruments on human trafficking and slavery, the rapid growth in human trafficking along with the process of globalisation at the dawn of the 21st century led states to realise the inadequacy of existing instruments to address the issue at global level. Accordingly, different countries and organisations adopted different definitions of trafficking based on their particular assumptions about the issue. Today, owing to proliferation of definitions, one of the main challenges to understand dynamics of human trafficking around the world is the lack of consensus on what counts as trafficking.

In this chapter, we briefly discuss four instruments of human trafficking: the first two are widely accepted across the world, whereas the last two are more specific to Pakistan.

I. The UN Protocol to Prevent, Suppress and Punish Trafficking in Persons, Especially Women and Children, Supplementing the United Nations Convention against Transnational Organised Crime (2000)

A generally agreed and broader definition of trafficking in persons is provided in Article 3 of the UN Protocol to Prevent, Suppress and Punish Trafficking in Persons, Especially Women and Children (2000).[22]

The Protocol defines trafficking as:

(a) The recruitment, transportation, transfer, harbouring or receipt of persons, by means of a threat or use of force or other forms of coercion, of abduction, of fraud, of deception, of the abuse of power or of a position of vulnerability, or of giving or receiving payments or benefits to achieve the consent of a person having control over another person for the purpose of exploitation. Exploitation shall include, at a minimum, the exploitation of the prostitution of others or other forms of sexual exploitation, forced labour or services, slavery or practices similar to slavery, servitude or the removal of organs;

(b) The consent of a victim of trafficking in persons to the intended exploitation set forth in subparagraph (a) of this article shall be irrelevant where any of the means set forth in subparagraph (a) have been used;

(c) The recruitment, transportation, transfer, harbouring or receipt of a child for the purpose of exploitation shall be considered "trafficking in persons" even if this does not involve any of the means set forth in subparagraph (a) of this article;

(d) "Child" shall mean any person under eighteen years of age.

The UN Protocol has three main aims: (a) to prevent and combat trafficking in persons; (b) to protect and assist the victims of trafficking; and, (c) to promote cooperation among states. According to UNODC (2006:12-13), while implementing the UN Trafficking Protocol, all countries should consider the following recommendations:

Prevention

1. To establish, together with NGOs and civil society, comprehensive regional and national policies and programmes to prevent and combat human trafficking and to protect the victims.
2. To implement, together with NGOs and civil society, research, information and media campaigns and social and economic initiatives to prevent and combat trafficking in persons.
3. To undertake measures to alleviate the vulnerability of people (women and children in particular) to human trafficking, such as poverty, underdevelopment and lack of equal opportunity.
4. To undertake measures to discourage demand that fosters exploitation that leads to trafficking in persons.
5. To provide training to relevant officials in the prevention, prosecution of trafficking in persons and protection of the rights of the victims.

6. To exchange information on human trafficking routes, modus operandi, traffickers profiles and victims identification.
7. To undertake measures to prevent means of transport operated by commercial carriers to be used in the commission of human trafficking offences.
8. To strengthen cooperation among border control agencies by, inter alia, establishing and maintaining direct channels of communication.

Prosecution

9. To undertake measures to ensure that travel and identity documents cannot easily be misused, falsified, unlawfully altered, replicated or issued; and to ensure the integrity and security of travel and identity documents and to prevent their unlawful creation, issuance and use.
10. To enact domestic laws making human trafficking a criminal offence. Such laws should also establish as criminal offences attempting to commit, participating as an accomplice, and organising or directing other persons to commit human trafficking.
11. To ensure such legislation applies to victims of all ages and both sexes; and clearly distinguish between trafficking in persons and other forms of irregular migration.
12. To ensure that the system of penalties is adequate, given the severity of the crime.
13. To protect the privacy and identity of victims in appropriate cases.
14. To establish measures to protect victims from revictimisation.
15. To implement measures providing to victims information on proceedings, assistance to enable their views and concerns to be presented and considered at appropriate stages of criminal proceedings.

16. To implement measures that offer victims the possibility of obtaining compensation.

Protection

17. To implement measures to provide for the physical, psychological and social recovery of victims. This should include housing and counselling in a language the victims can understand, medical, psychological and material assistance as well as employment, educational and training opportunities. The special needs of victims, in particular children, are to be taken into account.
18. To provide for the physical safety of victims following rescue.
19. To adopt measures that permit victims to remain in the territory, temporarily or permanently, in appropriate cases, giving consideration to humanitarian and compassionate factors.
20. To facilitate preferably voluntary return of the victim without undue or unreasonable delay, with due regard for the safety of the victim.

II. Trafficking Victims Protection Act (TVPA)

The United States has defined the severe forms of human trafficking in Sec. 103(8) of the Trafficking Victims Protection Act (2000) as:

A. sex trafficking in which a commercial sex act is induced by force, fraud, or coercion, or in which the person induced to perform such act has not attained 18 years of age; or
B. the recruitment, harbouring, transportation, provision, or obtaining of a person for labour or services, through the use of force, fraud, or coercion for the purpose of subjection to involuntary servitude, peonage, debt bondage, or slavery.[23]

The TVPA focuses on the three Ps (punishment, protection and prevention) to address the issue of human trafficking. Based on the definition of trafficking provided in the TVPA, the United States Department of State publishes an annual Trafficking in Persons Report (TIP Report) that provides the narratives of countries which are used as origin, transit, and destination for trafficking. The country narrative provides glimpse of the scope and nature of trafficking in a country, and highlights the government's efforts to combat trafficking and compliance with the minimum standards for the elimination of trafficking as laid out in the TVPA. In addition, the country narrative includes suggestions to combat trafficking. Based on the analysis of their situation, each country is rated as Tier 1, Tier 2, Tier 2 Watch List or Tier 3 (the 3-tier system has been explained in detail in chapter 2).

III. SAARC Convention on Preventing and Combating Trafficking in Women and Children for Prostitution (2002)

The member states of the South Asian Association for Regional Cooperation (SAARC)[24] including India, Pakistan, Bangladesh, Nepal, Sri Lanka, Bhutan, Maldives defined trafficking in Article 1(3) of the SAARC Convention on Preventing and Combating Trafficking in Women and Children for Prostitution in 2002.[25]

The Convention defines trafficking as:

> Trafficking means the moving, selling or buying of women and children for prostitution within and outside a country for monetary or other considerations with or without the consent of the person subjected to trafficking.

Furthermore, Article 1(2) of the Convention explains "Prostitution means the sexual exploitation or abuse of persons for commercial purposes".

IV. Prevention and Control of Human Trafficking Ordinance (P&CHTO), 2002

Pakistan has defined human trafficking in its Prevention and Control of Human Trafficking Ordinance (2002).[26]

According to Article 2(h) of the Ordinance:

> Human trafficking means obtaining, securing, selling, purchasing, recruiting, detaining, harbouring or receiving a person notwithstanding his implicit or explicit consent, by the use of coercion, kidnapping, abduction, or by giving or receiving any payment or benefit, or sharing or receiving a share for such person's subsequent transportation out of or into Pakistan by any means whatsoever for any of the purposes mentioned in section 3.

Further, Section 3 of the Ordinance states that the human trafficking shall be punishable as under:

(i) Whoever knowingly plans or executes any such plan for human trafficking into or out of Pakistan for the purpose of attaining any benefit, or for the purpose of exploitative entertainment, slavery or forced labour or adoption in or out of Pakistan shall be punishable with imprisonment which may extend to seven years and shall also be liable to fine:

Provided that in case of an accused who, in addition to committing an offence as aforesaid has also been guilty of kidnapping or abducting or any attempt thereto in connection with such offence, the imprisonment may extend to ten years with fine:

Provided further that whoever plans to commit an offence under this clause but has not as yet executed the same shall be punishable with a term of imprisonment, which may extend to five years and shall also be liable to fine.

(ii) Whoever knowingly provides, obtains or employs the labour or services of a person by coercion, scheme, plan or method intended to make such person believe that in the event of non-performance of such labour or service, he or any other person may suffer from serious harm or physical restraint or legal proceedings, shall be punishable with imprisonment which may extend to seven years and shall also be liable to fine:

Provided that if the commission of the offences under this clause involves kidnapping or abduction or any attempt thereto, the term of imprisonment may extend to ten years with fine:

Provided further that payment of any remuneration in lieu of services or labour of the victim shall not be treated as mitigating circumstance while awarding the punishment.

(iii) Whoever knowingly purchases, sells, harbours, transports, provides, detains or obtains a child or a woman through coercion, kidnapping or abduction, or by giving or receiving any benefit for trafficking him or her into or out of Pakistan or with intention thereof, for the purpose of exploitative entertainment by any person and has received or expects to receive some benefit in lieu thereof shall be punishable with imprisonment which may extend to ten years and shall also be liable to fine:

Provided that if the commission of the offence sunder this clause involves kidnapping or abduction or any attempt thereto of the victim, the term of imprisonment may extend to fourteen years with fine:

Provided further that plea, if any, taken by the biological parents of the child shall not prejudice the commission of offence under this clause.

(iv) Whoever knowingly takes, confiscates, possesses, conceals, removes or destroys any document related to human trafficking in furtherance of any offence committed under this Ordinance or to prevent or restrict or attempt to prevent or restrict, without lawful authority, a person's liberty to move or travel shall be punishable with imprisonment which may extend to seven years and shall also be liable to fine.

LIMITATIONS OF THE DEFINITIONS OF TRAFFICKING

The definitions of trafficking in the previous section reveal a lack of consensus on what constitutes as trafficking, though the attributes of trafficking reflect the interests and priorities of their promoters (Gallagher 2010). Although the UN Protocol was the first international document that—to a certain extent—reached a compromise over the definition of trafficking, still debates, arguments and confusions appear to be centred around the issues of consent, movement and purpose of trafficking (Rijken 2003; Sen and Nair 2005).

If we analyse these four definitions of human trafficking, we can identify three common elements of trafficking: movement, coercion and exploitation. Considering trafficking as a process, which should involve movement of persons, usually leads to the confusion of conceptualising trafficking as a form of (illegal) migration. It is important to reiterate that trafficking may not always involve physical movement—for instance in Amina's case. In cases of debt bondage or organ removal, persons could be subject to trafficking without necessarily required to move or move long distances. In case of organ removal, the person whose organ is removed does not move. Moreover, there is an unstated assumption about moving across national boundaries; consequently, trafficking continues to be considered as an issue of illegal migration—and national security—rather than illegal detention or exploitation. Trafficked persons, who are found to have used illicit means to migrate or have knowingly involved in illegal activities, are categorised as criminals who have violated immigration laws and deported to their home countries (Konrad 2008; Cameron and Newman 2008). Equally important is the fact that transnational trafficking may not always involve illegal migration as in some cases persons may be trafficked through legal migration. For example, in some cases traffickers marry young girls who then migrate with them as brides, but after reaching the point of destination they are sold or forced into slavery-like conditions (Skeldon 2000; Munir 2003). Therefore, restrictive immigration policies tend to further victimise vulnerable migrants, but have little effect on exploiters or controlling the menace of trafficking (Raymond 2002). Moreover, Sanghera (2005) argues that counter-trafficking interventions based on the conception of trafficking as a form of migration provide false solution to trafficking. This assumption about trafficking particularly restricts the movement of women and children who are considered to be vulnerable to trafficking. Hence, it reinforces gender-bias practices in the name of protecting women and children from exploitation.

The second common feature of the process of trafficking is coercion, but what counts as coercion is still not clear. Despite the fact that trafficking may occur with or without consent of the individual, law enforcement agencies tend to separate criminals and victims based on the criterion of consent and coercion. Consequently, anti-trafficking laws extend support to only those victims of trafficking who are believed to be forced into trafficking, whereas others remain outside their protective umbrella (Chapkis 2003). The issue becomes more problematic when trafficking involves initial consent of a trafficked person. For example, women who may enter into prostitution wilfully but later on are subject to exploitation and confinement, or in case of economic migrants who knowingly violate immigration laws but later on are subject to slavery-like conditions (Raymond 2002; Chapkis 2003; Bales 2005). Moreover, it is important to note that above definitions of trafficking and many others, fail to make a clear distinction between trafficking in women and children. Although women and children are more vulnerable to trafficking, clumping them together reinforces the assumption of considering women as childlike who cannot exercise their agency in making decisions and need 'protection' (Critelli 2010).

The third and the most important element of trafficking is exploitation. It is important to note that trafficking can still occur without movement or overt coercion, but it always involves exploitation of human beings. Identifying victims of trafficking and response to trafficking are, however, dominantly based on movement and coercion—rather than exploitation. Although the UN definition of trafficking exhibits an agreement that the purpose of trafficking is exploitation of human beings, still there are different explanations or interpretations regarding the nature of exploitation (e.g., the tendency to limit exploitation only to women's commercial sexual exploitation).

Many academics (e.g., Kempadoo 2005; Gallagher 2010; McCabe and Manian 2010) argue that one of the main reasons of failure to control the rapid growth of human trafficking is that response to trafficking tends to be shaped by the Western conceptualisation of human trafficking which ignores the ground realities in the global South, and do not necessarily address the root causes of the epidemic embedded in the global hegemonic structures of inequality. If we compare the UN protocol with the US protocol, some of these limitations are clear. The UN protocol emphasises prevention, prosecution and protection which is a significant step in identifying the three-pronged initiatives that are needed to address trafficking. This protocol goes beyond the governments, and draws in NGOs and civil societies as stakeholders in crafting preventative measures. However, some of the details written into these three facets are problematic. This protocol assumes societies are organised in much the same ways as Western countries and that ways of healing or protection depend on psychologists, counsellors, and trauma experts, resources that are extremely unlikely to be available for the victims like Salma or Asefa. Ultimately, as we mentioned earlier, the question of resource becomes important. In countries like Pakistan, financially burdened with national security measures, many of these resource provisions are not likely to be met.

The US standards provide a stark example of powerful protocols which are grounded in the need of a single country's interests and understanding. The TVPA primarily focuses on commercial sex trafficking and involuntary servitude. Most of the cases we presented would not be identified according to the TVPA indicators. All the countries are ranked based on their compliance with the TVPA's minimum standards, which are modelled on the US legislation rather than international human rights instruments (Gallagher 2010). As we asserted earlier in the chapter, the TVPA emphasises sex trafficking and forced labour without an associated attention to the rights that are violated, or not provided by the country to the victims. In the US's own case, recent labour upsurge in the country shows that despite the legality of their movement, their actual labour conditions reflect near-slavery conditions (Adur 2011). Yet these people would not fall within the purview of TVPA's indicators of a trafficked person. Moreover, the ranking of countries is not based on actual number of trafficked persons, but only on compliance with the TVPAs minimum standards. The data may be misleading since some countries with high prevalence of trafficking are ranked under Tier 1. As many scholars (e.g., Appadurai 1993; Nobles 2000; Kertzer and Arel 2002) have discussed with reference to Census and large-scale database, the power of countries or agencies to direct the terms for data collection has significant impact on the design and implementation of policies. Also, there is little attention paid to *markets* for trafficked people. Gathering those data, creating database that takes more comprehensive measure into account, to the extent possible, would bring more countries into the map of trafficking.

Victims of human trafficking include men, women and children. Since the emergence of the concept of trafficking, however, there has been a common assumption that the most widespread form of human trafficking is sex trafficking, which is supported by gender-bias explanations and statistics of trafficking (Chapkis 2003; Loff and Sanghera 2004). Accordingly, some academics (e.g., Brysk 2009; Wilson 2012) and the ILO (2014) have been arguing that trafficking for other purpose, for instance, exploitative labour is more common and widespread than the sex trafficking. Moral panic about prostitution and gendered assumptions about vulnerability to trafficking are still reflected in the definitions of trafficking which are subsequently translated into counter-trafficking interventions. For example, the title of the UN Protocol specifically focuses on trafficking in women and children. Similarly, the TVPA's explanation of severe forms of trafficking starts with sex trafficking with an unstated assumption that the majority of the trafficked individuals are women forced into prostitution who need to be rescued (Doezema 2002). While definitions of trafficking do acknowledge that men, women and children can be victims of trafficking, practically, very little is known about the vulnerabilities of men to trafficking. As the dominant focus of research on trafficking has been on women and children, hence statistics only demonstrate vulnerability of women and children to trafficking. Consequently, the focus of anti-trafficking interventions on women and children is justified by the identification that they comprise the majority of victims (Segrave *et al.* 2009).

Moreover, Chapkis (2003) notes that since emergence of the concept of trafficking, women involved in prostitution have been the main object of state regulation and control. For example, the TVPA distinguishes 'violated innocents' from 'illegal migrants' on the basis of gendered assumptions. Innocent victims of trafficking, assumed to be vulnerable women and children from other countries coerced into prostitution, are distinguished from economic migrants, believed to be men, who deliberately violate immigration laws for personal gain. Furthermore, support is extended to only those deserving victims who cooperate with the authorities in prosecuting traffickers. While this course of action appears to be the morally correct choice to make, a range of institutional arrangements structure impediments. The vulnerability of victims often increase in multiple ways so that the "choice" to leave and prosecute those who inflict violence is weighed, by victims, against the other realities of becoming illegal migrants or being branded as criminals, or lacking long term access to shelter, food, or the ability to move onto other spheres of life (Abraham 2000; Erturk and Purkayastha 2012).

Similar arguments can be made in case of the SAARC Convention that limits the scope of trafficking to the moving, selling or buying of women and children for prostitution for monetary or other considerations with or without the consent of the person subjected to trafficking. The Convention does not acknowledge other forms of trafficking, for example, trafficking for domestic servitude, debt bondage, forced labour, begging, organ removal and trafficking of children for exploitation as camel jockeys. Moreover, the focus of anti-trafficking interventions only on prostitution may increase victimisation of trafficked women through reinforcing the stigmatisation of all trafficked women as prostitutes (Asian Development Bank 2003). In 2004, the SAARC member states adopted *Five Points* to mutually address the issue of sexual exploitation and prostitution at the regional level.[27] The points include: (a) conduct better research into the demand that underpins sexual abuse and exploitation of children, including the abuse that results from home grown demand; (b) reinforce protection measures through the adoption of National Action Plans covering sexual abuse, exploitation and trafficking and these should be adequately funded; (c) develop compatible database of abused, exploited and trafficked children with information on age, gender and nationality that would allow better identification of national trends and indicators; (d) work with NGO, UN and multilateral partners to develop indicators of impact and effectiveness and identify successful initiatives and good practices; and, (e) work with children and young people to ensure their insights are included in policy formation and actions (Huda 2006). Till now, the regional states have, however, shown little commitment to implement or act upon these Five Points.

Moreover, Sanghera (2005) notes that trafficking laws tend to be based on certain assumptions rather than existing realities or experiences of the trafficked persons. Consequently, in spite of several national and international instruments of human trafficking and spending billions of dollars annually, estimates suggest that the phenomenon of trafficking is expanding rather rapidly. Although gender and human rights literatures on trafficking, as discussed in the previous chapters, do talk about structures that perpetrate vulnerability to trafficking, in practice, policies/laws are reduced to 'individual victims' and do not target structural inequalities. For example, definitions are usually reduced to women as victims of sexual exploitation without targeting the interplay of hegemonic structures that make those women vulnerable to exploitation. There is a disconnect between scholarship that talks about global political-economic structures and developing anti-trafficking policies which are reduced only to individual exeriences.

ANTI-TRAFFICKING LEGISLATION & INTERVENTIONS IN PAKISTAN

Pakistan has not yet signed the UN Protocol to Prevent, Suppress and Punish Trafficking in Persons, especially Women and Children. The Prevention and Control of Human Trafficking Ordinance (P&CHTO), entered into force in October 2002, is the most significant legislation in Pakistan to combat human trafficking, and provides the legal basis for anti-trafficking policies and interventions in the country (Haider 2005). Prior to this Ordinance, trafficking cases were tried under several other laws. For the implementation of P&CHTO, the government notified the Prevention and Control of Human Trafficking Rules in 2004. The main points of the

Rules include: (a) establishment of shelters, and security arrangements; (b) provision of services to the victims, including food and physical, psychological and legal assistance; (c) arrangements for repatriation of foreign victims of trafficking; and, the responsibilities of NGOs in provision of services to the victims of trafficking.

With the assistance of the IOM, Pakistan initiated implementing trafficking legislation and anti-trafficking interventions to curb the menace of human trafficking. The promulgation of the P&CHTO was a very significant step towards combating trafficking in Pakistan since it was the first time the government accepted that trafficking existed in the country. However, interviews with the stakeholders reveal that one of the key reasons that the government accepted the prevalence of trafficking in the country and introduced trafficking legislation was the fear of its ranking in the TIP Report, as the US funding/aid was contingent upon compliance with the TVPA's minimum standards. After initiating trafficking legislation, the ranking of Pakistan was improved from Tier 2 Watch List to Tier 2. Although the trafficking legislation in Pakistan was developed after reviewing trafficking related legislations in many other countries, it was not based on ground realities as it did not incorporate experiences of trafficked persons in the country.

There is no doubt that the passage of trafficking legislation in Pakistan is a commendable effort that reflects the commitment of the government to combat the menace of human trafficking. An analysis of the legislations, however, reveals several limitations that have serious implications in achieving the desired results. One of the main limitations of the P&CHTO is that it defines trafficking as a process that involves movement of person(s) into or out of Pakistan indicating that the Ordinance is silent on the issue of internal trafficking. Focusing only on international trafficking or separating it from internal trafficking reinforces the assumption that trafficking is a migration related crime rather than a human rights violation (Ray 2011). Consequently, law enforcement agencies usually confuse trafficking with human smuggling and there are no official disaggregated statistics of human trafficking and smuggling in Pakistan (TIP Report 2013). Cases of internal trafficking are tried under the Pakistan Penal Code or several other laws. However, one of the major implications of dealing with cases of trafficking as 'other offenses' is that they are usually less serious and carry mild sentences (Sanghera 2005). According to the TIP Report (2013), a large percentage of trafficking in Pakistan occurs within the country, and the country's largest human trafficking problem is bonded labour. As the internal trafficking is not covered under trafficking legislation in Pakistan, the Bonded Labour System (Abolition) Act (1992) deals with the cases of trafficking into bonded labour/debt bondage. According to the Act, "whoever compels other person for bonded/forced labour shall be punished with imprisonment for a term of at least 2 and maximum 5 years, or of fine of at least PKR 50,000, or both". Whereas, trafficking laws in Pakistan prescribe penalties between seven to fourteen years' imprisonment with fine if somebody is found involved in (transnational) trafficking, including trafficking into forced labour or debt bondage.

Moreover, trafficking laws in Pakistan are silent about traditional practices, such as *Walwar* (bride price), *Swara* (exchange of women in settling dispute), *Watta Satta* (exchange marriage) and forced/fake marriages that act as contributing factors in trafficking of women and girls. In many cases, *jirgas/ Panchayats* are also used to sanction crimes committed against women, especially trading them for settling disputes (Haider 2005; Hussein and Hussain 2012). The lack of understanding about the complex nature of trafficking process is a serious institutional constraint because trafficking cases are often not correctly identified, investigated, and prosecuted. As a result, many trafficked persons end up being criminalised. Also, owing to the fear of further victimisation by the police, many trafficked persons prefer not to contact the police or hesitate sharing information with them (Haider 2005).

Although several sections in the Prevention and Control of Human Trafficking Rules (2004) emphasise on the role of NGOs to address the issue of human trafficking in Pakistan, there is indeed weak coordination between NGOs and the government to share information and compliment each other's efforts. For example, Sections 4 & 5 of the Rules place great responsibility on NGOs regarding the provision of shelter for trafficked victims and their well being, and also propose inspection and cancellation of registration of the NGO or welfare organisation found involved in mistreating the victim. Moreover, the Pakistan Action Plan for Combating Human Trafficking (2005) highlights several measures to prevent human trafficking, including raising awareness and research and data collection to address the root causes of trafficking. The Action Plan, while acknowledging the severity of the problem in Pakistan, proclaims, "The subject of human trafficking is of immense importance for Pakistan since in our context the problem is multi-dimensional in nature being origin, transit and destination country. It has become critical to tackle this problem as it is one of the most serious organised crimes being committed in the country" (2005:1). Like trafficking legislation in Pakistan, the Action Plan, however, focuses only on transnational trafficking. Although the Federal Investigation Agency (FIA) has established Anti-trafficking Units (ATUs) at its headquarter and all Zonal Directorates to effectively address the issue of trafficking,[28] the ATUs tend to primarily combat trafficking as an issue of migration. Despite its limitations, the Action Plan provides a framework to address the issue of human trafficking in collaboration with the stakeholders. But, there has not been any study or report to document the implementation status of activities mentioned in the Action Plan. Owing to non-existence of any mechanism of community involvement, most of the people are not familiar with the concept of human trafficking. Some NGOs and research organisations, with the support of donor agencies, have conducted few studies on trafficking in different parts Pakistan, but still there has not been any comprehensive study at the national level to analyse the prevalence of various forms of trafficking in the country. As a result, magnitude and nature of trafficking remain unknown in Pakistan, and anti-trafficking interventions continue to be based on assumptions rather than lived experiences of trafficked persons. After the 18th Constitutional Amendment in Pakistan in 2010, subjects like health, labour, education, social welfare and women development have been devolved to provincial level. Now greater responsibility lies on the provincial governments to initiate legislation and counter-trafficking interventions to curb the menace of trafficking in Pakistan.

INSTITUTIONAL SUPPORT FOR VICTIMS OF TRAFFICKING IN PAKISTAN

According to the P&CHTO and its Rules, the government, in collaboration with NGOs, is responsible to provide secure shelter and other services to victims of trafficking. The analysis of trafficking laws, however, demonstrates that provision of these services is not available to every victim of trafficking, but it depends on certain assumptions about the process of trafficking and deserving victims. For example, Article 6 (iii) of the P&CHTO requires the "Government to make arrangements for the shelter, food, and medical treatment of victim being an unaccompanied child or a destitute woman". Thus, under the Ordinance, the state is not responsible to provide such services to men who are victims of trafficking. This reflects the assumption that only women and children could be vulnerable to trafficking, and therefore, need state protection, whereas men, who are considered to be involved in smuggling and illegal migration, should be interrogated in detention centres. However, this assumption is not unique to Pakistan because such practices exist in other (developing and developed) countries as well. For example, a survey of shelter beds for survivors of human trafficking in the US conducted by the Polaris Project in 2012 showed that while there were total 529 shelter beds exclusively designated for human trafficking survivors, only two were exclusively earmarked for male survivors of trafficking.[29]

Furthermore, as per trafficking legislation in Pakistan, a model shelter for foreign victims of trafficking was established in Islamabad during 2005-2006 with the support of the IOM and the US Embassy. The shelter was run by the IOM who also developed Standard Operating Procedures to manage shelters for victims of trafficking. It was expected that the government will establish such type of shelters in other parts of the country as well. However, after a couple of years, as funding of the project—under which the IOM was running the shelter—was exhausted, the only exclusively designated shelter for the victims of trafficking was also closed. Despite spending a lot of money on the model shelter, the government could not sustain the project through its own resources, mainly due to 'lack of funds'. And, recalling the details about Salma or Amina, it is clear that victims like these two girls would not be admitted to these shelters.

Although the trafficking legislation and the National Action Plan for Combating Human Trafficking require the government to establish special shelters for victims of trafficking where they could be provided secure accommodation and other services, no such designated shelter exists in Pakistan. However, already existing shelters for women, which were established by the government for victims of violence, are now dealing with the cases of trafficking as well. As these shelters were not established for victims of trafficking, the management of shelters have not received any training as to how to identify and deal with the victims of trafficking. Considering trafficked persons as runaway or homeless persons lead to the assumption that victims of trafficking do not have any special needs, and fails to understand series of exploitation, trauma and health issues (e.g., HIV/AIDS) associated with trafficking (Finklea, Fernandes-Alcantara and Siskin 2011). The issue may become more severe in case of foreign victims of trafficking who cannot speak or understand local language. Moreover, due to lack of awareness and training, the management of shelters is usually not capable of identifying trafficking victims. As a result, trafficked persons are registered under other forms of violence and exploitation, and their rights as trafficked persons remain unaddressed (Enterprise for Business & Development Management 2009).

In addition, interviews with the management of the shelters reveal several constraints and challenges being faced while managing the shelters. For example, regular cut in the budget of shelters makes it really difficult for the management to provide adequate services to the residents, including clothing, food, and health and legal services. Therefore, they usually depend on NGOs or philanthropists who could support activities of the shelters or provide free medico-legal assistance. Although some international organisations are working for the betterment of the shelters, the basic responsibility to facilitate the management of the shelters in providing better services to the residents lies with the government (Hahmi 2009). Owing to increasing number of women who experience violence and leave their homes, shelters in big cities are usually overcrowded. For example, in some shelters there were more than 80 residents against the maximum capacity of 50 persons.

Moreover, as these shelters are established to provide temporary accommodation, women are generally allowed to stay there for a specific (short) time period. Owing to the existence of strong patriarchal norms, a woman who leaves her home and seeks state protection is usually considered responsible for bringing bad name to her family's honour. Consequently, in many cases families disown such women or refuse to accept them, which significantly increase their vulnerability to trafficking. In addition, owing to inadequate rehabilitation strategies, victims are motivated to reconcile with their families and relatives who might be the main perpetrators of violence. To recall the case of Amina, her brothers were waiting for her to complete her term at the shelter. In this case, they would bring her back home, but exactly for the opposite purposes to what 'going home' is supposed to mean. There are some reported cases where on return the victims were killed by their family members (Amin 2010).

A Superintendent of shelter shares her experience and concern over this situation as:

> Women who come to the shelter are victims of several forms of violence. In the majority of cases, either families don't want to have contact with the victims, who are blamed to bringing bad name to their families, or victims don't want to go back to their families/communities because their own relatives are involved in their exploitation, and they fear that they will be killed by them. Thus, women who do not have any place to go become easy prey to traffickers who lure these women through fake promise of employment or marriage.

As mentioned earlier, one of the serious limitations of the existing shelters is that they do not have any strong mechanism for rehabilitation of victims of trafficking. Trafficked women are usually uneducated and lack economic resources. Although shelters offer trainings in basic skills (e.g., knitting, embroidery) so that the victims could economically support themselves, unfortunately, these skills rarely provide them employment or an income that is adequate to live on. As a result, many victims of exploitation who have been *rescued* and trained in basic skills for earning a living often end up in the same exploitative situations wherefrom they are rescued. Especially in South Asia, due to strong stigmatisation of prostitution and the lack of community involvement in anti-trafficking efforts, rehabilitation or integration of victims of sex trafficking into their communities remains the most challenging—and often neglected—task (Brown 2000, Asian Development Bank 2003).

CHAPTER 6

Combating Human Trafficking: Looking at the Future

Only when human sorrows are turned into a toy with glaring colours will baby people become interested—for a while at least. The people are a very fickle baby that must have new toys every day. The 'righteous' cry against the white slave traffic is such a toy. It serves to amuse the people for a little while, and it will help to create a few more fat political jobs—parasites who stalk about the world as inspectors, investigators, detectives etc.

What really is the cause of the trade in women? Not merely white women, but yellow and black women as well. Exploitation, of course: the merciless Moloch of capitalism that fattens on underpaid labour, thus driving thousands of women and girls into prostitution. With Mrs. Warren these girls feel, "Why waste your life working for a few shillings a week in a scullery, eighteen hours a day?"

Goldman (1910:2)

Ms Mam's stories were told in interviews with journalists . . . she attracted high-profile supporters . . . there were benefits [event] thrown . . . Ms Mam's target audience of well-off Westerners, eager to do good,

> often knows little about the sex trade. It does not require much for them to imagine all women who sell sex as victims are in need of rescue . . . When [a group] . . . arrived . . . to film sex workers . . . [this activist] told the Asian Correspondent News site that this approach was part of the problem: You show the face of the mother who is so poor she had to sell her daughter for money? How does this help the daughter or the mother? It doesn't . . .. Ending abuse in sex trade requires action that is less telegenic than a photo op or gala . . .. [a] hero like Ms Mam lets those who lift her up feel like they are heroes too. They can be saviours simply by repeating her stories and swiping their cards. Now Ms Mam has been exposed before her donors and the Western media who anointed her and made fighting sex trafficking a kind of industry in itself, while sex workers suffered the consequences.
>
> Grant (2014, A27)

We represent a section of a quotation we highlighted in chapter 1, and also highlight a more recent argument. Separated by more than a century, both quotes point to some similar features showing our inability to address some of the root causes of trafficking and exploitation. Human trafficking continues within and across countries, regions and continents. Despite the significant political, economic, technological changes that have occurred over the 20th century, yet we continue to focus on trafficking for sex only. Our zeal for rescue mission continues, and fighting trafficking has become a kind of industry itself without actually addressing the deeper causes that 'make' a victim. Despite several international instruments on human trafficking, anti-trafficking programmes have done little to control the rapid growth of the phenomenon worldwide.

In chapter one, and throughout this discourse, we discussed the problems with the definitions and data on trafficking.

Many are *estimates* for the purpose of indicating the magnitude of the problem; many of the estimates are developed for validating sex trafficking of innocent female victims to brothels. It is surprising to note that despite the growing literature on human trafficking, especially during the last decade, very few studies on trafficking are actually based on the lived experiences of the trafficked persons. The possibility of multiple episodes of trafficking that occur during a trafficked victim's life are mostly absent from the discourse. Consequently, when incomplete understandings of trafficking are translated into policies and practice, they remain inadequate to address the phenomenon effectively (Brysk and Choi-Fitzpatrick 2012).

In order to understand the complex nature of trafficking as we glimpsed from the narratives of Salma, Amina, Yasmin, Asefa, Abbas, Rahman and Usman, we need to highlight multiple vulnerabilities that provide opportunities to powerful traffickers to prey on the weak. Although academic literature on trafficking highlights structural factors that perpetuate vulnerability to trafficking, in practice, counter-trafficking policies and interventions are reduced to (individual level) victims who need to be saved from (individual level) traffickers. Thus, we assess the need to understand as to how the phenomenon of trafficking is deeply intertwined in intersections of global and local political-economic structures and power relations that create repeated cycles of vulnerability for some segments of population. As trafficking occurs within interlocking systems of political, economic and social exploitation, it cannot be studied as a discrete occurrence of violence unrelated to other ongoing structural violence and exploitation. It is not only poverty that exposes people to trafficking, but it is indeed victims' helplessness in terms of political-economic-social empowerment to resist deceptions of the traffickers. As a result of these multiple causes and cycles of vulnerability, trafficking cannot be addressed as one-time phenomenon only through humanitarian or other interventions.

We also pointed out the need to go beyond the conflation of gender with women in the definitions of trafficking. Scholarly literatures primarily focusing on women also acknowledged the importance of the intersections of race/ gender/class/age structures which shape the lives of different groups of men and women in diverse relations of power and political subordination. By insisting on the need to move beyond the conflation of gender with women, we do not intend to divert our attention from female victims. The reality is that more women and girls are affected by trafficking. We would argue that more accurate representations of the female and male victims—the intersecting gender/class/age and other structures that shape their lives—are likely to lead to more useful solutions and increase the efficacy of anti-trafficking initiatives. At the same time, we have to address the race-based stereotypes about hapless women victims (and predatory men) in Asia and Africa that appear to drive many of the most prominent international conversations about trafficking. Here, we presented poor men who acted upon norms of family honour—their roles as bread winners—and sell their kidneys to pay for inherited and present debt. We met women and girls, who, despite impossible odds, ran away to shelters. The central gender issue here is whether there is accurate understanding of their problems and concerted efforts to provide supportive solutions.

The experiences of victims of trafficking, including the brief accounts we presented in this book, suggest many factors that enhance vulnerability of people to trafficking. These include structural factors such as political and economic instability, armed conflicts, poverty, gender-based violence, diminishing employment opportunities, lack of legal and social protection which are shaped by interactions of local and global political-economic systems. Globalisation and neo-liberal economic policies have produced increased level of inequalities and disparities within and between states. Therefore, instead of focusing on individual level victims and perpetrators, discussion on trafficking should include larger policy debates on the consequences of globalisation, regional conflicts and the resource drain from the developing world that diminish the ability of states to protect their citizens (Bertone 2000; Sen and Nair 2005; Cameron and Newman 2008; Shelley 2010; Kara 2011). Moreover, it is important to note that political-economic structures and individual level experiences are not static; they change over time and space. For example, though trafficking is a cross-country issue, every country has its own specific context that aids perpetuation of particular forms of trafficking. Therefore, anti-trafficking initiatives should take into account this dynamic nature of structures and individual experiences.

Moreover, instead of investing so much of time and effort into 'rescue approaches', efforts should be focused more on empowering socially, economically and politically marginalised groups to extricate themselves from the cycles of vulnerability and exploitation. Since emergence of the concept of trafficking, the dominant focus of anti-trafficking interventions has been on rescuing women trafficked into prostitution which has, however, failed to address the root causes of trafficking in human beings manifested in diverse forms of exploitation. Grant's (2014) article, which is partially quoted at the beginning of this chapter, highlights the problems of the current emphases to stop trafficking. Benefit galas are arranged, news is created and sold, money is raised, but the root causes are not addressed. Featuring the stories of poor women does not help most women escape cycles of poverty and violence; these efforts may help a few victims but the effect does not 'trickle down' unless the root causes are addressed. But, it is not simply the benign outcomes—*some* victims are rescued—that are of concern to us. Organising activism and anti-trafficking initiatives in this way imply that the funds are not donated towards less newsworthy, but principled efforts to alleviate the everyday suffering of millions of people. The slogan of *Veshya Anyay Mukti Parishad*

(VAMP), a collective of sex workers in India, best describes the limitations of rescue approach as "Save us from our saviours. We are tired of being saved" (cited in Seshu and Bandhopadhyay 2009:14). Moreover, as vulnerabilities to trafficking are shaped by intersections of local and global structures of inequality, imported "individualistic rehabilitation model" and "welfarist programmes" may not assist in addressing the issue of power inequalities. Counter-trafficking interventions need to be based on existing ground realities and the lived experiences of victims of trafficking to bring the desired social change (Kempadoo 2005; Chowdhury 2011).

We also pointed out that a major reason of the failure to effectively address the issue of human trafficking is the tendency of governments to consider trafficking as an issue of crime against state rather than as an issue of human rights violations. Consequently, immigration laws are made more restrictive to control human trafficking. This, in turn, motivates unskilled and poor people to explore illicit means and become prey to traffickers and exploiters. Unless governments protect the lives of their citizens and improve their socioeconomic status, the over-reliance on restrictive immigration policies is unlikely to deal with the magnitude of transnational trafficking (Skeldon 2000; Segrave *et al.* 2009; Shelley 2010). Moreover, experiences of different countries suggest that reliance upon traditional law enforcement strategies is not adequate to combat human trafficking. There is a need to enhance community participation and awareness, especially in zones of political and economic instability and poverty-stricken regions which tend to be the main recruiting centres.

Drawing upon the gendered human rights approach, we emphasised a need to revisit trafficking as an issue of *human security*. Our argument, throughout this book, to examine the multiple linked causes of trafficking is consistent with the approach developed by Tripp, Ferree and Ewig (2013) on human security and violence. Tripp and her colleagues emphasise the connections between macro and micro forms of violence—between violence through prolonged conflict and violence within private spheres—and gendered inequalities. The cases we highlighted here show how gendered inequalities—intersectional inequalities that include men and women—are enhanced in contexts of prolonged violence. Coupled with limited opportunities for accessing living wages, education, shelter, healthcare or the substantive political rights to organise for better conditions of life—all of which were evident in the narratives of Salma, Amina, Yasmin, Asefa, Abbas, Rahman and Usman—people are vulnerable to be trafficked *repeatedly within a person's life course, though not for the same purpose, and not in the same way*. Trafficked victims and people vulnerable to trafficking need more initiatives to ensure their access to the entire range of human rights.

Understanding this larger frame of trafficking leads us to argue that the limited scope of definitions/understanding of trafficking results in denying rights to trafficked persons and increase the chances of their re-victimisation. Despite some limitations, the UN Protocol to Prevent, Suppress and Punish Trafficking in Persons, Especially Women and Children is the first wide-ranging international agreement that provides a broad framework to deal with the issue of trafficking on a global level through mutual collaboration (Raymond 2002). The question for us is whether regional—single country or groups of countries—states can use the UN Protocol as the base and *add* structural factors *that exist in their region* as causes of trafficking to develop more effective and comprehensive database (and understandings) of trafficking. At the same time, these efforts will have to use existing local cultural and structural resources and develop new ones that can be mobilised to mitigate and ultimately eradicate trafficking.

As we reflect on these definitions and challenges, and read thousands of words of many protocols and policies we presented here, we are still struck by the relative scarcity of victims' accounts of what make them vulnerable to trafficking and what they see as solutions to their life-conditions. If we need to go beyond the current rescue initiatives, their views ought to play some part in devising anti-trafficking solutions.

Thus, we end this book with the words of some of the trafficked victims that best express the urgency of finding better solutions.

> "They asked me to go back with them, but I refused them. They threatened me that once I leave the shelter, they would cut me into pieces."
>
> "I ran away from home and came to the shelter. I don't know where to go and what will happen to me in future."
>
> "We sell our body to protect honour of our women . . . We do it because we are helpless and do not have any other option."

Notes

1 http://www.unicefusa.org/assets/pdf/End-Child-Trafficking-One-Pager.pdf

2 Punjab is the most populous province of Pakistan with approximately 55.6% of the total population of the country (http://pwd.punjab.gov.pk/). As a province of Pakistan, this region encapsulates the legal and policy context of Pakistan. Trafficked women were interviewed in shelters, established by Government of the Punjab, in various districts of the province. Whereas, trafficked men were interviewed in district Sargodha where trafficking into debt bondage/forced labour and organ trade is widespread (Naqvi *et al* 2007). In order to protect the respondents' confidentiality, we have neither used their names nor location of the shelters.

3 http://www.unicefusa.org/assets/pdf/End-Child-Trafficking-One-Pager.pdf

4 See for instance, *Robinson Takes On Trafficking,* (www.cambodiadaily.com/archive/robinson-takes-on-trafficking-34137/)

5 http://www.unodc.org/unodc/treaties/CTOC/

6 The region of South Asia consists of eight countries, including India, Pakistan, Bangladesh, Nepal, Bhutan, Sri Lanka, Maldives, and Afghanistan.

7 http://www.nab.gov.bt/ActParliament/25PCB_4_upload.pdf

8 http://www.hsph.harvard.edu/population/trafficking/nepal.trafficking.07.pdf

9 http://hrcsl.lk/PFF/LIbrary_Domestic_Laws/Legislations_related%20_to_Migrants_Workers/Penal%20Code%20(Amendment)%20Act,%20No.%2016%20of%202006.pdf

10 South Asian Association for Regional Cooperation (SAARC) was established on December 8, 1985. The region is home to nearly 1.5 billion people or approximately 22% of world's population. (http://www.saarc-sec.org/Charter-Day/6/).

11 http://www.ivap.org.pk/Home.aspx

12 We discuss the problems of the shelters later.

13 Karachi is the capital of Sindh province in Pakistan.
14 We think this is an overly generalised stereotype and have written elsewhere to refute such over generalisation (See Narayan and Purkayastha: *Living Our Religions*, 2009).
15 United Nations. *The Universal Declaration of Human Rights: A Living Document* (http://www.un.org/en/events/humanrightsday/udhr60/declaration.shtml)
16 The Constitution of the Islamic Republic of Pakistan (as modified up to 28 February, 2012) http://www.na.gov.pk/uploads/documents/1333523681_951.pdf.
17 http://www1.umn.edu/humanrts/instree/whiteslavetraffic1904.html
18 http://www1.umn.edu/humanrts/instree/whiteslavetraffic1910.html
19 https://treaties.un.org/Pages/ViewDetails.aspx?src=TREATY&mtdsg_no=VII-2&chapter=7&lang=en
20 http://www.oas.org/juridico/mla/en/traites/en_traites-inter-women_1933.pdf
21 http://www.ohchr.org/EN/ProfessionalInterest/Pages/TrafficInPersons.aspx
22 http://www.unodc.org/documents/treaties/UNTOC/Publications/TOC%20Convention/TOCebook-e.pdf
23 http://www.state.gov/documents/organization/10492.pdf
24 Afghanistan became member of the SAARC in April 2007 at the Fourteenth SAARC Summit in Delhi (http://saarc-sec.org/Charter-Day/6/).
25 http://www.saarc-sec.org/userfiles/conv-traffiking.pdf
26 http://www.fia.gov.pk/pchto2002.htm
27 (http://www.unicef.org/media/media_23509.html)
28 http://www.fia.gov.pk/dep_trafficking.htm
29 Shelter Beds for Human Trafficking Survivors in the United States (http://www.polarisproject.org/resources/tools-for-service-providers-and-law-enforcement/shelter-bed-report)
30 http://www.ohchr.org/Documents/Publications/Traffickingen.pdf
31 The term "trafficking", as used in the present Principles and Guidelines, refers to the recruitment, transportation, transfer, harbouring or receipt of persons, by means of the threat or use of force or other forms of coercion, of abduction, of fraud, of deception, of the abuse of power or of a position of vulnerability or of the giving or receiving of payments or benefits to achieve the consent of a person having control over another person, for the purpose of exploitation. Exploitation shall include, at a minimum, the exploitation of the prostitution of others or other forms of sexual exploitation, forced labour or services, slavery or practices similar to slavery, servitude or the removal of organs. Source: Protocol to Prevent, Suppress and

Punish Trafficking in Persons, Especially Women and Children, supplementing the United Nations Convention against Transnational Organised Crime (article 3 (a)).

32 For the purposes of the present Principles and Guidelines, the "component acts" and "component offences" of trafficking are understood to include the recruitment, transportation, transfer, harbouring or receipt of persons over eighteen years of age by means of threat, force, coercion or deception for the purpose of exploitation. The recruitment, transportation, transfer, harbouring or receipt of a person under eighteen years of age constitute component acts and component offences of trafficking in children. Source: Protocol to Prevent, Suppress and Punish Trafficking in Persons, Especially Women and Children, supplementing the United Nations Convention against Transnational Organised Crime, articles 3 (a) and 3 (c).

33 For the purposes of the present Principles and Guidelines, conduct and offences "related to" trafficking are understood to include: exploitation of the prostitution of others or other forms of sexual exploitation, forced labour or services, slavery or practices similar to slavery and servitude. Source: Protocol to Prevent, Suppress and Punish Trafficking in Persons, Especially Women and Children, supplementing the United Nations Convention against Transnational Organised Crime, article 3 (a).

34 The human rights treaty-monitoring bodies include the Human Rights Committee; the Committee on Economic, Social and Cultural Rights; the Committee on the Elimination of Discrimination against Women; the Committee on the Elimination of Racial Discrimination; the Committee against Torture; and the Committee on the Rights of the Child.

35 The term "traffickers", where it appears in the present Principles and Guidelines, is used to refer to: recruiters; transporters; those who exercise control over trafficked persons; those who transfer and/or maintain trafficked persons in exploitative situations; those involved in related crimes; and those who profit either directly or indirectly from trafficking, its component acts and related offences.

36 The Protocol to Prevent, Suppress and Punish Trafficking in Persons, Especially Women and Children (Palermo Protocol), supplementing the United Nations Convention against Transnational Organised Crime, defines trafficking in persons as: "... the recruitment, transportation, transfer, harbouring or receipt of persons, by means of the threat or use of force or other forms of coercion, of abduction, of fraud, of deception, of the abuse of power or of a position of vulnerability or of the giving or receiving of payments or benefits to achieve the consent of a person having control over another person

for the purpose of exploitation. Exploitation shall include, at a minimum, the exploitation of the prostitution of others or other forms of sexual exploitation, forced labour or services, slavery or practices similar to slavery, servitude or the removal of organs (article 3 (a)). The Protocol further states that the recruitment, transportation, transfer, harbouring or receipt of a child for the purpose of exploitation shall be considered "trafficking in persons" even if this does not involve any of the means set forth above (article 3 (c)).

37 Federal Investigation Agency, Government of Pakistan (http://www.fia.gov.pk/pchto2002.htm)

38 Federal Investigation Agency, Government of Pakistan (http://www.fia.gov.pk/pchto2002.htm)

39 http://www.saarc-sec.org/userfiles/conv-traffiking.pdf

APPENDIX A
Recommended Principles and Guidelines on Human Rights and Human Trafficking[30]

RECOMMENDED PRINCIPLES ON HUMAN RIGHTS AND HUMAN TRAFFICKING[31]

The primacy of human rights

1. The human rights of trafficked persons shall be at the centre of all efforts to prevent and combat trafficking and to protect, assist and provide redress to victims.
2. States have a responsibility under international law to act with due diligence to prevent trafficking, to investigate and prosecute traffickers and to assist and protect trafficked persons.
3. Anti-trafficking measures shall not adversely affect the human rights and dignity of persons, in particular the rights of those who have been trafficked, and of migrants, internally displaced persons, refugees and asylum-seekers.

Preventing trafficking

4. Strategies aimed at preventing trafficking shall address demand as a root cause of trafficking.
5. States and intergovernmental organisations shall ensure that their interventions address the factors that increase vulnerability to trafficking, including inequality, poverty and all forms of discrimination.
6. States shall exercise due diligence in identifying and eradicating public-sector involvement or complicity in trafficking. All public officials suspected of being implicated

in trafficking shall be investigated, tried and, if convicted, appropriately punished.

Protection and assistance

7. Trafficked persons shall not be detained, charged or prosecuted for the illegality of their entry into or residence in countries of transit and destination, or for their involvement in unlawful activities to the extent that such involvement is a direct consequence of their situation as trafficked persons.
8. States shall ensure that trafficked persons are protected from further exploitation and harm and have access to adequate physical and psychological care. Such protection and care shall not be made conditional upon the capacity or willingness of the trafficked person to cooperate in legal proceedings.
9. Legal and other assistance shall be provided to trafficked persons for the duration of any criminal, civil or other actions against suspected traffickers. States shall provide protection and temporary residence permits to victims and witnesses during legal proceedings.
10. Children who are victims of trafficking shall be identified as such. Their best interests shall be considered paramount at all times. Child victims of trafficking shall be provided with appropriate assistance and protection. Full account shall be taken of their special vulnerabilities, rights and needs.
11. Safe (and, to the extent possible, voluntary) return shall be guaranteed to trafficked persons by both the receiving State and the State of origin. Trafficked persons shall be offered legal alternatives to repatriation in cases where it is reasonable to conclude that such repatriation would pose a serious risk to their safety and/or to the safety of their families.

Criminalisation, punishment and redress

12. States shall adopt appropriate legislative and other measures necessary to establish, as criminal offences, trafficking, its component acts[32] and related conduct.[33]
13. States shall effectively investigate, prosecute and adjudicate trafficking, including its component acts and related conduct, whether committed by governmental or by non-State actors.

14. States shall ensure that trafficking, its component acts and related offences constitute extraditable offences under national law and extradition treaties. States shall cooperate to ensure that the appropriate extradition procedures are followed in accordance with international law.
15. Effective and proportionate sanctions shall be applied to individuals and legal persons found guilty of trafficking or of its component or related offences.
16. States shall, in appropriate cases, freeze and confiscate the assets of individuals and legal persons involved in trafficking. To the extent possible, confiscated assets shall be used to support and compensate victims of trafficking.
17. States shall ensure that trafficked persons are given access to effective and appropriate legal remedies.

RECOMMENDED GUIDELINES ON HUMAN RIGHTS AND HUMAN TRAFFICKING

Guideline 1: Promotion and protection of human rights

Violations of human rights are both a cause and a consequence of trafficking in persons. Accordingly, it is essential to place the protection of all human rights at the centre of any measures taken to prevent and end trafficking. Anti-trafficking measures should not adversely affect the human rights and dignity of persons and, in particular, the rights of those who have been trafficked, migrants, internally displaced persons, refugees and asylum-seekers.

States and, where applicable, intergovernmental and non-governmental organisations, should consider:

1. Taking steps to ensure that measures adopted for the purpose of preventing and combating trafficking in persons do not have an adverse impact on the rights and dignity of persons, including those who have been trafficked.
2. Consulting with judicial and legislative bodies, national human rights institutions and relevant sectors of civil society in the development, adoption, implementation and review of anti-trafficking legislation, policies and programmes.

3. Developing national plans of action to end trafficking. This process should be used to build links and partnerships between governmental institutions involved in combating trafficking and/or assisting trafficked persons and relevant sectors of civil society.
4. Taking particular care to ensure that the issue of gender-based discrimination is addressed systematically when anti-trafficking measures are proposed with a view to ensuring that such measures are not applied in a discriminatory manner.
5. Protecting the right of all persons to freedom of movement and ensuring that anti-trafficking measures do not infringe upon this right.
6. Ensuring that anti-trafficking laws, policies, programmes and interventions do not affect the right of all persons, including trafficked persons, to seek and enjoy asylum from persecution in accordance with international refugee law, in particular through the effective application of the principle of non-refoulement.
7. Establishing mechanisms to monitor the human rights impact of anti-trafficking laws, policies, programmes and interventions. Consideration should be given to assigning this role to independent national human rights institutions where such bodies exist. Non-governmental organisations working with trafficked persons should be encouraged to participate in monitoring and evaluating the human rights impact of anti-trafficking measures.
8. Presenting detailed information concerning the measures that they have taken to prevent and combat trafficking in their periodic reports to the United Nations human rights treaty-monitoring bodies.[34]
9. Ensuring that bilateral, regional and international cooperation agreements and other laws and policies concerning trafficking in persons do not affect the rights, obligations or responsibilities of States under international law, including human rights law, humanitarian law and refugee law.
10. Offering technical and financial assistance to States and relevant sectors of civil society for the purpose of

developing and implementing human rights-based anti-trafficking strategies.

Guideline 2: Identification of trafficked persons and traffickers

Trafficking means much more than the organised movement of persons for profit. The critical additional factor that distinguishes trafficking from migrant smuggling is the presence of force, coercion and/or deception throughout or at some stage in the process—such deception, force or coercion being used for the purpose of exploitation. While the additional elements that distinguish trafficking from migrant smuggling may sometimes be obvious, in many cases they are difficult to prove without active investigation. A failure to identify a trafficked person correctly is likely to result in a further denial of that person's rights. States are therefore under an obligation to ensure that such identification can and does take place.

States are also obliged to exercise due diligence in identifying traffickers,[35] including those who are involved in controlling and exploiting trafficked persons.

States and, where applicable, intergovernmental and non-governmental organisations, should consider:

1. Developing guidelines and procedures for relevant State authorities and officials such as police, border guards, immigration officials and others involved in the detection, detention, reception and processing of irregular migrants, to permit the rapid and accurate identification of trafficked persons.
2. Providing appropriate training to relevant State authorities and officials in the identification of trafficked persons and correct application of the guidelines and procedures referred to above.
3. Ensuring cooperation between relevant authorities, officials and non-governmental organisations to facilitate the identification and provision of assistance to trafficked persons. The organisation and implementation of such cooperation should be formalised in order to maximise its effectiveness.

4. Identifying appropriate points of intervention to ensure that migrants and potential migrants are warned about possible dangers and consequences of trafficking and receive information that enables them to seek assistance if required.
5. Ensuring that trafficked persons are not prosecuted for violations of immigration laws or for the activities they are involved in as a direct consequence of their situation as trafficked persons.
6. Ensuring that trafficked persons are not, in any circumstances, held in immigration detention or other forms of custody.
7. Ensuring that procedures and processes are in place for receipt and consideration of asylum claims from both trafficked persons and smuggled asylum seekers and that the principle of non-refoulement is respected and upheld at all times.

Guideline 3: Research, analysis, evaluation and dissemination

Effective and realistic anti-trafficking strategies must be based on accurate and current information, experience and analysis. It is essential that all parties involved in developing and implementing these strategies have and maintain a clear understanding of the issues.

The media has an important role to play in increasing public understanding of the trafficking phenomenon by providing accurate information in accordance with professional ethical standards.

States and, where appropriate, intergovernmental and non-governmental organisations, should consider:

1. Adopting and consistently using the internationally agreed definition of trafficking contained in the Palermo Protocol.[35]
2. Standardising the collection of statistical information on trafficking and related movements (such as migrant smuggling) that may include a trafficking element.
3. Ensuring that data concerning individuals who are trafficked is disaggregated on the basis of age, gender, ethnicity and other relevant characteristics.

4. Undertaking, supporting and bringing together research into trafficking. Such research should be firmly grounded in ethical principles, including an under-standing of the need not to re-traumatise trafficked persons. Research methodologies and interpretative techniques should be of the highest quality.
5. Monitoring and evaluating the relationship between the intention of anti-trafficking laws, policies and interventions, and their real impact. In particular, ensuring that distinctions are made between measures which actually reduce trafficking and measures which may have the effect of transferring the problem from one place or group to another.
6. Recognising the important contribution that survivors of trafficking can, on a strictly voluntary basis, make to developing and implementing anti-trafficking interventions and evaluating their impact.
7. Recognising the central role that non-governmental organisations can play in improving the law enforcement response to trafficking by providing relevant authorities with information on trafficking incidents and patterns taking into account the need to preserve the privacy of trafficked persons.

Guideline 4: Ensuring an adequate legal framework

The lack of specific and/or adequate legislation on trafficking at the national level has been identified as one of the major obstacles in the fight against trafficking. There is an urgent need to harmonise legal definitions, procedures and cooperation at the national and regional levels in accordance with international standards. The development of an appropriate legal framework that is consistent with relevant international instruments and standards will also play an important role in the prevention of trafficking and related exploitation.

States should consider:

1. Amending or adopting national legislation in accordance with international standards so that the crime of trafficking

is precisely defined in national law and detailed guidance is provided as to its various punishable elements. All practices covered by the definition of trafficking such as debt bondage, forced labour and enforced prostitution should also be criminalised.

2. Enacting legislation to provide for the administrative, civil and, where appropriate, criminal liability of legal persons for trafficking offences in addition to the liability of natural persons. Reviewing current laws, administrative controls and conditions relating to the licensing and operation of businesses that may serve as cover for trafficking such as marriage bureaux, employment agencies, travel agencies, hotels and escort services.
3. Making legislative provision for effective and proportional criminal penalties (including custodial penalties giving rise to extradition in the case of individuals). Where appropriate, legislation should provide for additional penalties to be applied to persons found guilty of trafficking in aggravating circumstances, including offences involving trafficking in children or offences committed or involving complicity by State officials.
4. Making legislative provision for confiscation of the instruments and proceeds of trafficking and related offences. Where possible, the legislation should specify that the confiscated proceeds of trafficking will be used for the benefit of victims of trafficking. Consideration should be given to the establishment of a compensation fund for victims of trafficking and the use of confiscated assets to finance such a fund.
5. Ensuring that legislation prevents trafficked persons from being prosecuted, detained or punished for the illegality of their entry or residence or for the activities they are involved in as a direct consequence of their situation as trafficked persons.
6. Ensuring that the protection of trafficked persons is built into anti-trafficking legislation, including protection from summary deportation or return where there are reasonable grounds to conclude that such deportation or return would represent a significant security risk to the trafficked person and/or her/his family.

7. Providing legislative protection for trafficked persons who voluntarily agree to cooperate with law enforcement authorities, including protection of their right to remain lawfully within the country of destination for the duration of any legal proceedings.
8. Making effective provision for trafficked persons to be given legal information and assistance in a language they understand as well as appropriate social support sufficient to meet their immediate needs. States should ensure that entitlement to such information, assistance and immediate support is not discretionary but is available as a right for all persons who have been identified as trafficked.
9. Ensuring that the right of trafficking victims to pursue civil claims against alleged traffickers is enshrined in law.
10. Guaranteeing that protections for witnesses are provided for in law.
11. Making legislative provision for the punishment of public sector involvement or complicity in trafficking and related exploitation.

Guideline 5: Ensuring an adequate law enforcement response

Although there is evidence to suggest that trafficking in persons is increasing in all regions of the world, few traffickers have been apprehended. More effective law enforcement will create a disincentive for traffickers and will therefore have a direct impact upon demand.

An adequate law enforcement response to trafficking is dependent on the cooperation of trafficked persons and other witnesses. In many cases, individuals are reluctant or unable to report traffickers or to serve as witnesses because they lack confidence in the police and the judicial system and/or because of the absence of any effective protection mechanisms. These problems are compounded when law enforcement officials are involved or complicit in trafficking. Strong measures need to be taken to ensure that such involvement is investigated, prosecuted and punished. Law enforcement officials must also be sensitised to the paramount requirement of ensuring the safety of trafficked persons. This responsibility lies with the investigator and cannot be abrogated.

States and, where applicable, intergovernmental and non-governmental organisations should consider:

1. Sensitising law enforcement authorities and officials to their primary responsibility to ensure the safety and immediate well-being of trafficked persons.
2. Ensuring that law enforcement personnel are provided with adequate training in the investigation and prosecution of cases of trafficking. This training should be sensitive to the needs of trafficked persons, particularly those of women and children, and should acknowledge the practical value of providing incentives for trafficked persons and others to come forward to report traffickers. The involvement of relevant non-governmental organisations in such training should be considered as a means of increasing its relevance and effectiveness.
3. Providing law enforcement authorities with adequate investigative powers and techniques to enable effective investigation and prosecution of suspected traffickers. States should encourage and support the development of proactive investigatory procedures that avoid over-reliance on victim testimony.
4. Establishing specialist anti-trafficking units (com-prising both women and men) in order to promote competence and professionalism.
5. Guaranteeing that traffickers are and will remain the focus of anti-trafficking strategies and that law enforcement efforts do not place trafficked persons at risk of being punished for offences committed as a consequence of their situation.
6. Implementing measures to ensure that "rescue" operations do not further harm the rights and dignity of trafficked persons. Such operations should only take place once appropriate and adequate procedures for responding to the needs of trafficked persons released in this way have been put in place.
7. Sensitising police, prosecutors, border, immigration and judicial authorities, and social and public health workers

to the problem of trafficking and ensuring the provision of specialised training in identifying trafficking cases, combating trafficking and protecting the rights of victims.

8. Making appropriate efforts to protect individual trafficked persons during the investigation and trial process and any subsequent period when the safety of the trafficked person so requires. Appropriate protection programmes may include some or all of the following elements: identification of a safe place in the country of destination; access to independent 1egal counsel; protection of identity during legal proceedings; identification of options for continued stay, resettlement or repatriation.
9. Encouraging law enforcement authorities to work in partnership with non-governmental agencies in order to ensure that trafficked persons receive necessary support and assistance.

Guideline 6: Protection and support for trafficked persons

The trafficking cycle cannot be broken without attention to the rights and needs of those who have been trafficked. Appropriate protection and support should be extended to all trafficked persons without discrimination.

States and, where applicable, intergovernmental and non-governmental organisations, should consider:

1. Ensuring, in cooperation with non-governmental organisations, that safe and adequate shelter that meets the needs of trafficked persons is made available. The provision of such shelter should not be made contingent on the willingness of the victims to give evidence in criminal proceedings. Trafficked persons should not be held in immigration detention centres, other detention facilities or vagrant houses.
2. Ensuring, in partnership with non-governmental organisations, that trafficked persons are given access to primary health care and counselling. Trafficked persons should not be required to accept any such support and assistance and they should not be subject to mandatory testing for diseases, including HIV/AIDS.

3. Ensuring that trafficked persons are informed of their right of access to diplomatic and consular representatives from their State of nationality. Staff working in embassies and consulates should be provided with appropriate training in responding to requests for information and assistance from trafficked persons. These provisions would not apply to trafficked asylum-seekers.
4. Ensuring that legal proceedings in which trafficked persons are involved are not prejudicial to their rights, dignity or physical or psychological well-being.
5. Providing trafficked persons with legal and other assistance in relation to any criminal, civil or other actions against traffickers/exploiters. Victims should be provided with information in a language that they understand.
6. Ensuring that trafficked persons are effectively protected from harm, threats or intimidation by traffickers and associated persons. To this end, there should be no public disclosure of the identity of trafficking victims and their privacy should be respected and protected to the extent possible, while taking into account the right of any accused person to a fair trial. Trafficked persons should be given full warning, in advance, of the difficulties inherent in protecting identities and should not be given false or unrealistic expectations regarding the capacities of law enforcement agencies in this regard.
7. Ensuring the safe and, where possible, voluntary return of trafficked persons and exploring the option of residency in the country of destination or third-country resettlement in specific circumstances (e.g. to prevent reprisals or in cases where re-trafficking is considered likely).
8. In partnership with non-governmental organisations, ensuring that trafficked persons who do return to their country of origin are provided with the assistance and support necessary to ensure their well-being, facilitate their social integration and prevent re-trafficking. Measures should be taken to ensure the provision of appropriate physical and psychological health care, housing and educational and employment services for returned trafficking victims.

Guideline 7: Preventing trafficking

Strategies aimed at preventing trafficking should take into account demand as a root cause. States and intergovernmental organisations should also take into account the factors that increase vulnerability to trafficking, including inequality, poverty and all forms of discrimination and prejudice. Effective prevention strategies should be based on existing experience and accurate information.

States, in partnership with intergovernmental and non-governmental organisations and where appropriate, using development cooperation policies and programmes, should consider:

1. Analysing the factors that generate demand for exploitative commercial sexual services and exploitative labour and taking strong legislative, policy and other measures to address these issues.
2. Developing programmes that offer livelihood options, including basic education, skills training and literacy, especially for women and other traditionally disadvantaged groups.
3. Improving children's access to educational opportunities and increasing the level of school attendance, in particular by girl children.
4. Ensuring that potential migrants, especially women, are properly informed about the risks of migration (e.g. exploitation, debt bondage and health and security issues, including exposure to HIV/AIDS) as well as avenues available for legal, non-exploitative migration.
5. Developing information campaigns for the general public aimed at promoting awareness of the dangers associated with trafficking. Such campaigns should be informed by an understanding of the complexities surrounding trafficking and of the reasons why individuals may make potentially dangerous migration decisions.
6. Reviewing and modifying policies that may compel people to resort to irregular and vulnerable labour migration. This process should include examining the effect on women of repressive and/or discriminatory nationality, property, immigration, emigration and migrant labour laws.
7. Examining ways of increasing opportunities for legal, gainful and non-exploitative labour migration. The

promotion of labour migration by the State should be dependent on the existence of regulatory and supervisory mechanisms to protect the rights of migrant workers.

8. Strengthening the capacity of law enforcement agencies to arrest and prosecute those involved in trafficking as a preventive measure. This includes ensuring that law enforcement agencies comply with their legal obligations.
9. Adopting measures to reduce vulnerability by ensuring that appropriate legal documentation for birth, citizenship and marriage is provided and made available to all persons.

Guideline 8: Special measures for the protection and support of child victims of trafficking

The particular physical, psychological and psychosocial harm suffered by trafficked children and their increased vulnerability to exploitation require that they be dealt with separately from adult trafficked persons in terms of laws, policies, programmes and interventions. The best interests of the child must be a primary consideration in all actions concerning trafficked children, whether undertaken by public or private social welfare institutions, courts of law, administrative authorities or legislative bodies. Child victims of trafficking should be provided with appropriate assistance and protection and full account should be taken of their special rights and needs.

States and, where applicable, intergovernmental and non-governmental organisations, should consider, in addition to the measures outlined under Guideline 6:

1. Ensuring that definitions of trafficking in children in both law and policy reflect their need for special safeguards and care, including appropriate legal protection. In particular, and in accordance with the Palermo Protocol, evidence of deception, force, coercion, etc. should not form part of the definition of trafficking where the person involved is a child.
2. Ensuring that procedures are in place for the rapid identification of child victims of trafficking.
3. Ensuring that children who are victims of trafficking are not subjected to criminal procedures or sanctions for offences related to their situation as trafficked persons.

4. In cases where children are not accompanied by relatives or guardians, taking steps to identify and locate family members. Following a risk assessment and consultation with the child, measures should be taken to facilitate the reunion of trafficked children with their families where this is deemed to be in their best interest.
5. In situations where the safe return of the child to his or her family is not possible, or where such return would not be in the child's best interests, establishing adequate care arrangements that respect the rights and dignity of the trafficked child.
6. In both the situations referred to in the two paragraphs above, ensuring that a child who is capable of forming his or her own views enjoys the right to express those views freely in all matters affecting him or her, in particular concerning decisions about his or her possible return to the family, the views of the child being given due weight in accordance with his or her age and maturity.
7. Adopting specialised policies and programmes to protect and support children who have been victims of trafficking. Children should be provided with appropriate physical, psychosocial, legal, educational, housing and health-care assistance.
8. Adopting measures necessary to protect the rights and interests of trafficked children at all stages of criminal proceedings against alleged offenders and during procedures for obtaining compensation.
9. Protecting, as appropriate, the privacy and identity of child victims and taking measures to avoid the dissemination of information that could lead to their identification.
10. Taking measures to ensure adequate and appropriate training, in particular legal and psychological training, for persons working with child victims of trafficking.

Guideline 9: Access to remedies

Trafficked persons, as victims of human rights violations, have an international legal right to adequate and appropriate remedies. This right is often not effectively available to trafficked persons as they frequently lack information on the possibilities and processes for obtaining remedies, including compensation, for trafficking and related exploitation. In order to overcome this problem, legal and other material assistance should be provided to trafficked persons to enable them to realise their right to adequate and appropriate remedies.

States and, where applicable, intergovernmental and non-governmental organisations, should consider:

1. Ensuring that victims of trafficking have an enforceable right to fair and adequate remedies, including the means for as full a rehabilitation as possible. These remedies may be criminal, civil or administrative in nature.
2. Providing information as well as legal and other assistance to enable trafficked persons to access remedies. The procedures for obtaining remedies should be clearly explained in a language that the trafficked person understands.
3. Making arrangements to enable trafficked persons to remain safely in the country in which the remedy is being sought for the duration of any criminal, civil or administrative proceedings.

Guideline 10: Obligations of peacekeepers, civilian police and humanitarian and diplomatic personnel

The direct or indirect involvement of peacekeeping, peace-building, civilian policing, humanitarian and diplomatic personnel in trafficking raises special concerns. States, intergovernmental and non-governmental organisations are responsible for the actions of those working under their authority and are therefore under an obligation to take effective measures to prevent their nationals and employees from engaging in trafficking and related exploitation. They are also required to investigate thoroughly all allegations of trafficking and related exploitation and to provide for and apply appropriate sanctions to personnel found to have been involved in trafficking.

States and, where appropriate, intergovernmental and non-governmental organisations, should consider:

1. Ensuring that pre- and post-deployment training programmes for all peacekeeping, peace-building, civilian policing, humanitarian and diplomatic staff adequately address the issue of trafficking and clearly set out the expected standard of behaviour. This training should be developed within a human rights framework and delivered by appropriately experienced trainers.
2. Ensuring that recruitment, placement and transfer procedures (including those of private contractors and sub-contractors) are rigorous and transparent.
3. Ensuring that staff employed in the context of peace-keeping, peace-building, civilian policing, humanitarian and diplomatic missions do not engage in trafficking and related exploitation or use the services of persons in relation to which there are reasonable grounds to suspect they may have been trafficked. This obligation also covers complicity in trafficking through corruption or affiliation with any person or group of persons who could reasonably be suspected of engaging in trafficking and related exploitation.
4. Developing and adopting specific regulations and codes of conduct setting out expected standards of behaviour and the consequences of failure to adhere to these standards.
5. Requiring all personnel employed in the context of peacekeeping, peace-building, civilian policing, humanitarian and diplomatic missions to report on any instances of trafficking and related exploitation that come to their attention.
6. Establishing mechanisms for the systematic investigation of all allegations of trafficking and related exploitation involving personnel employed in the context of peacekeeping, peace-building, civilian policing, humanitarian and diplomatic missions.
7. Consistently applying appropriate criminal, civil and administrative sanctions to personnel shown to have engaged in or been complicit in trafficking and related exploitation. Intergovernmental and non-governmental organisations should, in appropriate cases, apply disciplinary sanctions to staff members found to be involved in trafficking and related exploitation in addition to and

independently of any criminal or other sanctions decided on by the State concerned. Privileges and immunities attached to the status of an employee should not be invoked in order to shield that person from sanctions for serious crimes such as trafficking and related offences.

Guideline 11: Cooperation and coordination between States and regions

Trafficking is a regional and global phenomenon that cannot always be dealt with effectively at the national level: a strengthened national response can often result in the operations of traffickers moving elsewhere. International, multilateral and bilateral cooperation can play an important role in combating trafficking activities. Such cooperation is particularly critical between countries involved in different stages of the trafficking cycle.

States and, where applicable, intergovernmental and non-governmental organisations, should consider:

1. Adopting bilateral agreements aimed at preventing trafficking, protecting the rights and dignity of trafficked persons and promoting their welfare.
2. Offering, either on a bilateral basis or through multilateral organisations, technical and financial assistance to States and relevant sectors of civil society for the purpose of promoting the development and implementation of human rights-based anti-trafficking strategies.
3. Elaborating regional and sub-regional treaties on trafficking, using the Palermo Protocol and relevant international human rights standards as a baseline and framework.
4. Adopting labour migration agreements, which may include provision for minimum work standards, model contracts, modes of repatriation, etc., in accordance with existing international standards. States are encouraged effectively to enforce all such agreements in order to help eliminate trafficking and related exploitation.
5. Developing cooperation arrangements to facilitate the rapid identification of trafficked persons including the sharing and exchange of information in relation to their nationality and right of residence.

6. Establishing mechanisms to facilitate the exchange of information concerning traffickers and their methods of operation.
7. Developing procedures and protocols for the conduct of proactive joint investigations by law enforcement authorities of different concerned States. In recognition of the value of direct contacts, provision should be made for direct transmission of requests for assistance between locally competent authorities in order to ensure that such requests are rapidly dealt with and to foster the development of cooperative relations at the working level.
8. Ensuring judicial cooperation between States in investigations and judicial processes relating to trafficking and related offences, in particular through common prosecution methodologies and joint investigations. This cooperation should include assistance in: identifying and interviewing witnesses with due regard for their safety; identifying, obtaining and preserving evidence; producing and serving the legal documents necessary to secure evidence and witnesses; and the enforcement of judgements.
9. Ensuring that requests for extradition for offences related to trafficking are dealt with by the authorities of the requested State without undue delay.
10. Establishing cooperative mechanisms for the confiscation of the proceeds of trafficking. This cooperation should include the provision of assistance in identifying, tracing, freezing and confiscating assets connected to trafficking and related exploitation.
11. Exchanging information and experience relating to the implementation of assistance, return and integration programmes with a view to maximising impact and effectiveness.
12. Encouraging and facilitating cooperation between non-governmental organisations and other civil society organisations in countries of origin, transit and destination. This is particularly important to ensure support and assistance to trafficked persons who are repatriated.

APPENDIX B

Prevention and Control of Human Trafficking Ordinance, 2002[37]

An ORDINANCE to Prevent and Control Human Trafficking

WHEREAS the offences relating to traffic in human beings are incompatible with the dignity and worth of human being and endanger the welfare of the individual, the family and the community.

AND WHEREAS it is expedient and necessary to provide effective measures to prevent offences related to human trafficking and to protect and assist victims of such trafficking.

AND WHEREAS the President is satisfied that circumstances exist which render it necessary to take immediate action.

NOW, THEREFORE, in pursuance of the Proclamation of Emergency of the fourteenth day of October, 1999, and the Provisional Constitution Order No. 1 of 1999, read with the Provisional Constitution (Amendment) Order No. 9 of 1999, and in exercise of all powers enabling him in that behalf, the President of the Islamic Republic of Pakistan is pleased to make and promulgate the following Ordinance:

1. Short title, extent and commencement.
   (1) This Ordinance may be called the Prevention and Control of Human Trafficking Ordinance, 2002.
   (2) It extends to the whole of Pakistan.
   (3) It shall come into force at once.

2. Definition. In this Ordinance, unless there is anything repugnant in the subject or context.
   (a) "benefit" includes monetary profit, proceeds or payment in cash or in kind.

(b) "child" means any person who has not attained the age of eighteen years.
(c) "Code" means the Code of Criminal Procedure, 1898 (Act V of 1898).
(d) "coercion" means the use of force, violence, physical restraint, deception, fraud or acts or circumstances not necessarily including physical force but calculated to have the same effect, such as the credible threat of force or of infliction of serious harm.
(e) "document" related to human trafficking includes a passport, a travel documents and any identification document used by law enforcement authorities.
(f) "exploitative entertainment" means all activities in connection with human sports or sexual practices or sex and related abusive practices.
(g) "Government" means the Federal Government.
(h) "human trafficking" means obtaining, securing, selling, purchasing, recruiting, detaining, harbouring or receiving a person, notwithstanding his implicit or explicit consent, by the use of coercion, kidnapping, abduction, or by giving or receiving any payment or benefit, or sharing or receiving a share for such person's subsequent transportation out of or into Pakistan by any means whatsoever for any of the purposes mentioned in section 3.
(i) "inhuman sports" include all sports involving, as a matter of normal course, infliction of physical or mental injury on a person against his will, intention or reasonable expectation.
(j) "organised criminal group" means a structured group of two or more persons, existing for a period of time and acting in concert with the aim of committing any offence under this Ordinance, in order to obtain, directly or indirectly, any financial or other material benefit and includes a person knowingly receiving or disbursing benefits accruing from the commission of any offence in relation to human trafficking by an organised criminal group; and
(k) "victim" means the person who is the subject of or against whom any offence under this Ordinance has been committed.

3. Punishment for human trafficking. The human trafficking shall be punishable as under.

   (i) Whoever knowingly plans or executes any such plan for human trafficking into or out of Pakistan for the purpose of attaining any benefit, or for the purpose of exploitative entertainment, slavery or forced labour or adoption in or out of Pakistan shall be punishable with imprisonment which may extend to seven years and shall also be liable to fine: Provided that in case of an accused who, in addition to committing an offence as aforesaid has also been guilty of kidnapping or abducting or any attempt thereto in connection with such offence, the imprisonment may extend to ten years with fine:

   Provided further that whoever plans to commit an offence under this clause but has not as yet executed the same shall be punishable with a term of imprisonment, which may extend to five years and shall also be liable to fine.

   (ii) Whoever knowingly provides, obtains or employs the labour or services of a person by coercion, scheme, plan or method intended to make such person believe that in the event of non-performance of such labour or service, he or any other person may suffer from serious harm or physical restraint or legal proceedings, shall be punishable with imprisonment which may extend to seven years and shall also be liable to fine:

   Provided that if the commission of the offences under this clause involves kidnapping or abduction or any attempt thereto, the term of imprisonment may extend to ten years with fine:

   Provided further that payment of any remuneration in lieu of services or labour of the victim shall not be treated as mitigating circumstance while awarding the punishment.

   (iii) Whoever knowingly purchases, sells, harbours, transports, provides, detains or obtains a child or a woman through coercion, kidnapping or abduction, or by giving or receiving any benefit for trafficking him or her into or out of Pakistan or with intention thereof, for the purpose of exploitative entertainment by any person and has received or expects to receive some benefit in lieu thereof shall be punishable with imprisonment which may extend to ten years and shall also be liable to fine:

Provided that if the commission of the offence sunder this clause involves kidnapping or abduction or any attempt thereto of the victim, the term of imprisonment may extend to fourteen years with fine:

Provided further that plea, if any, taken by the biological parents of the child shall not prejudice the commission of offence under this clause.

(iv) Whoever knowingly takes, confiscates, possesses, conceals, removes or destroys any document related to human trafficking in furtherance of any offence committed under this Ordinance or to prevent or restrict or attempt to prevent or restrict, without lawful authority, a person's liberty to move or travel shall be punishable with imprisonment which may extend to seven years and shall also be liable to fine.

4. Offences committed by organised criminal groups. —Where an organised criminal group is guilty of any offence under clauses (i), (ii), (iii) or (iv) of section 3, the term of imprisonment or each member of such group involved in the commission of such offence shall not be less than ten years imprisonment and may extend to fourteen years where the purpose of trafficking of a victim is exploitative entertainment and shall also be liable to fine.

5. Repetition of commission of offences. —Whoever repeats the commission of an offence under this Ordinance, the term of imprisonment may extend to fourteen years and the off under shall also be liable to fine.

6. Compensation to the victim. The court trying an offence under this Ordinance may where appropriate direct:

(i) The competent authorities of the Government, at any stage of the trial to allow or extend the stay of the victim in Pakistan till such time, as the court deems necessary.

(ii) Payment of compensation and expenses to the victim in accordance with section 545 of the Code.

(iii) Government to make arrangements for the shelter, food and medical treatment of victim being an unaccompanied child or a destitute woman.

7. Proceedings under the Ordinance to be in addition to and not in derogation of any other law. The proceedings under the Ordinance shall be in addition to and not in derogation of any other proceedings initiated under any other law for the time being in force.
8. Offences to be cognisable etc. All offences under the Ordinance shall be cognisable, non bail able, and non-compoundable as construed by the Code.
9. Investigation. Notwithstanding anything contained in the Code or any other law for the time being in force, the investigation of the offences under the Ordinance shall be carried out by only such persons or agencies as are specially empowered by the Government in that behalf.
10. Cognisance of offences etc. No court inferior to that of a Magistrate of the First Class shall try an offence punishable under this Ordinance. Notwithstanding anything contained in section 32 of the Code, it shall be lawful for a Magistrate of the First Class to pass any sentence authorised by this Ordinance.
11. Indemnity. No suit, prosecution or any other legal proceedings shall lie against the Government or any other person exercising any power or performing any function under this Ordinance or the rules made there under for anything done in good faith.
12. Power to make rules. The Government may, by a notification in official gazette, make rules to carry out the purposes of this Ordinance.

GENERAL PERVEZ MUSHARRAF
President

Mr JUSTICE MANSOOR AHMED
Secretary

APPENDIX C

Prevention and Control of Human Trafficking Rules, 2004[38]

ISLAMABAD, 29 NOVEMBER 2004

S.R.O.970 (1)/2004_ In exercise of powers conferred by section 12 of the Prevention and Control of Human Trafficking Ordinance, 2002, (LIX of 2002), the Federal Government is pleased to make the following rules, namely:

1. Short title and commencement
   (1) These rules may be called the Prevention and Control of Human Trafficking Rules, 2004.
   (2) They shall come into force at once.

2. Definitions. In these Rules, unless there is anything repugnant in the subject or context.
   (1) (a) "court" means the court having jurisdiction to try the offences under the Ordinance.
   (b) "Government" means the Federal Government.
   (c) "Non-Governmental Organisations" means the Non-Governmental Organisations notified by the Government under these rules from time to time.
   (d) "Ordinance" means the Prevent and Control of Human Trafficking Ordinance 2002 (LIX of 2002); and
   (e) "victim" shall have the same meaning as defined in the Ordinance.
   (2) Words and expression used but not defined in these rules shall have the same meaning as in the Ordinance.

3. Recording statement and custody of the victim.
   (1) A victim of an offence under the Ordinance, shall be produced before the court for recording his statement

under section 164 of the Code of Criminal Procedure, 1998 (V of 1998), except where the victim is unable, or otherwise not feasible for any reason to be recorded in writing, to get his statement recorded.

(2) In case the victim is an un-accompanied child or a destitute women, the court before whom such victim is produced may pass an order to keep him in a shelter home established by the Government or by the Non-Government Organisations for accommoda-tion, food and medical treatment.

Provided that where the victim is not satisfied with the Non-Governmental Organisation to which his custody was given by the court, he may apply to the court for alternate shelter.

(3) The court may, for the welfare of the victim, hand over the custody to any of his blood relation after requiring a bound from the custodian for safe c custody of the victim and his production before the court at the time and place mentioned in the bond and shall continue to produce until otherwise directed.

4. Establishment of shelter homes and security arrangements. — The Government shall establish shelter homes for safe custody of the victims and shall also make necessary security arrangement for the protection of the victims in the shelter homes whether established by the Government or the Non-Governmental Organisations.

5. Responsibilities of Non-Governmental Organisations.

(1) The Non-Governmental Organisations to which the victims are handed over, shall be responsible for proper shelter, food and medical treatment at a notified place which shall be open to inspection by an inspecting officer notified by the Government.

(2) In case any Non-Governmental Organisation is found involved in maltreatment with the victim or fails to fulfil its responsibilities of providing proper shelter, food and medical treatment, its notification may e cancelled, after giving an opportunity of being heard.

6. Legal assistance to the victim.
   (1) The Government shall and the Non-Governmental Organisations may provide necessary legal assistance to the victim during trial of the case and other legal proceedings under the Ordinance.
   (2) The Government shall allocate appropriate funds for providing legal assistance to the victims.

7. Recording evidence and repatriation of the victim
   (1) Where a victim is not a citizen of Pakistan, the court shall record the evidence of the victim at the earliest. If the victim is no more required for the trial, the court may direct the Government to facilitate such victim for this repatriation.
   Provided that the victim whose presence is considered necessary by the court for the trial of the case or his immediate repatriation is not possible, shall be entitled to apply to the National Alien Registration Authority for his temporary registration as alien or for work permit.
   (2) If the repatriation of the victim is decided, the Government shall in consultation with the concerned Embassy or, as the case may be, the High Commission of the country to which the victim belongs, make necessary arrangements for its safe return.
   (3) The Non-Governmental Organisations may provide assistance to the Government in the process of repatriation of the victim.
   (4) The Government shall establish special funds for repatriation of the victim.
   (5) The Government shall establish special funds for preparation of the victim [Ministry of Interior No.13/54/2002-FIA (PO)].

MRS AMNA IMRAN KHAN
Deputy Secretary (FIA)

APPENDIX D

SAARC Convention on Preventing and Combating Trafficking in Women and Children for Prostitution[39]

THE MEMBER STATES OF THE SOUTH ASIAN ASSOCIATION FOR REGIONAL COOPERATION (SAARC), PARTIES TO THE PRESENT CONVENTION

EMPHASISING that the evil of trafficking in women and children for the purpose of prostitution is incompatible with the dignity and honour of human beings and is a violation of basic human rights;

RECALLING the decision of the Ninth SAARC Summit (May, 1997) that the feasibility of a regional Convention to combat the grave crime of trafficking in women and children for prostitution should be explored;

RECALLING ALSO the relevant international legal instruments relating to prevention of trafficking in women and children, including the Convention for the Suppression of Trafficking in Persons and of the Exploitation of Prostitution of Others, 1949; Convention on the Elimination of all Forms of Discrimination against Women, 1979; International Covenant on Civil and Political Rights, 1966; and the Convention on the Rights of the Child, 1989;

GIVING due regard to the implementation of the recommendations of the various pertinent International Bodies and Conferences including the Fourth World Conference on Women at Beijing (1995);

NOTING with concern the increasing exploitation by traffickers of women and children from SAARC countries and their increasing use of these countries as sending, receiving and transit points;

RECOGNISING in this regard the importance of establishing effective regional cooperation for preventing trafficking for prostitution and for investigation, detection, interdiction, prosecution and punishment of those responsible for such trafficking;

EMPHASISING the need to strengthen cooperation in providing assistance, rehabilitation and repatriation to victims of trafficking for prostitution;

HAVE AGREED as follows:

ARTICLE I: DEFINITIONS

For the purpose of this Convention:

1) "Child" means a person who has not attained the age of 18 years;
2) "Prostitution" means the sexual exploitation or abuse of persons for commercial purposes;
3) "Trafficking" means the moving, selling or buying of women and children for prostitution within and outside a country for monetary or other considerations with or without the consent of the person subjected to trafficking;
4) "Traffickers" means persons, agencies or institutions engaged in any form of trafficking;
5) "Persons subjected to trafficking" means women and children victimised or forced into prostitution by the traffickers by deception, threat, coercion, kidnapping, sale, fraudulent marriage, child marriage, or any other unlawful means;
6) "Protective home" means a home established or recognised by a Government of a Member State for the reception, care, treatment and rehabilitation of rescued or arrested persons subjected to trafficking;
7) "Repatriation" means return to the country of origin of the person subjected to trafficking across international frontiers.

ARTICLE II: SCOPE OF THE CONVENTION

The purpose of this Convention is to promote cooperation amongst Member States so that they may effectively deal with the various aspects of prevention, interdiction and suppression of trafficking in women and children; the repatriation and rehabilitation of victims of trafficking and prevent the use of women and children in international prostitution networks, particularly where the countries of the SAARC region are the countries of origin, transit and destination.

ARTICLE III: OFFENCES

1. The State Parties to the Convention shall take effective measures to ensure that trafficking in any form is an offence under their respective criminal law and shall make such an offence punishable by appropriate penalties which take into account its grave nature.
2. The State Parties to the Convention, in their respective territories, shall provide for punishment of any person who keeps, maintains or manages or knowingly finances or takes part in the financing of a place used for the purpose of trafficking and knowingly lets or rents a building or other place or any part thereof for the purpose of trafficking.
3. Any attempt or abetment to commit any crime mentioned in paras 1 and 2 above or their financing shall also be punishable.

ARTICLE IV: AGGRAVATING CIRCUMSTANCES

1. The State Parties to the Convention shall ensure that their courts having jurisdiction over the offences committed under this Convention, can take into account factual circumstances which make the commission of such offences particularly grave, viz.

a) the involvement in the offences of an organised criminal group to which the offender belongs;
b) the involvement of the offender in other international organised criminal activities;
c) the use of violence or arms by the offender;
d) the fact that the offender holds a public office and that the offence is committed in misuse of that office;
e) the victimisation or trafficking of children;
f) the fact that the offence is committed in a custodial institution or in an educational institution or social facility or in their immediate vicinity or in other places to which children and students visit for educational, sports, social and cultural activities;
g) previous conviction, particularly for similar offences, whether in a Member State or any other country.

ARTICLE V: JUDICIAL PROCEEDINGS

In trying offences under this Convention, judicial authorities in Member States shall ensure that the confidentiality of the child and women victims is maintained and that they are provided appropriate counselling and legal assistance.

ARTICLE VI: MUTUAL LEGAL ASSISTANCE

1. The State Parties to the Convention shall grant to each other the widest measure of mutual legal assistance in respect of investigations, inquiries, trials or other proceedings in the requesting State in respect of offences under this Convention. Such assistance shall include:
   a) taking of evidence and obtaining of statements of persons;
   b) provision of information, documents and other records including criminal and judicial records;
   c) location of persons and objects including their identification;
   d) search and seizures;
   e) delivery of property including lending of exhibits;

f) making detained persons and others available to give evidence or assist investigations;
g) service of documents including documents seeking attendance of persons; and
h) any other assistance consistent with the objectives of this Convention.

2. Requests for assistance shall be executed promptly in accordance with their national laws and in the manner requested by the Requesting State. In the event that the Requested State is not able to comply in whole or in part with a request for assistance or decides to postpone execution it shall promptly inform the Requesting State and shall give reasons for the same.

ARTICLE VII: EXTRADITION OR PROSECUTION

1. The offences referred to in the present Convention shall be regarded as extraditable offences in any extradition treaty which has been or may hereinafter be concluded, between any of the Parties to the Convention.
2. If a State Party which makes extradition conditional on the existence of a treaty, receives a request for extradition from another State Party with which it has no extradition treaty, the Requested State shall, if so permitted by its laws, consider this Convention as the basis for extradition in respect of the offences set forth in Article III.
3. Extradition shall be granted in accordance with the laws of the State to which the request is made.
4. The State Party in whose territory the alleged offender is present shall, if it does not extradite him or her, submit, without exception whatsoever and without undue delay, the case to its competent authorities for the purpose of prosecution in accordance with the laws of that State.
5. In States where extradition of their nationals is not permitted under their law, nationals who have committed offences under the present Convention shall be prosecuted and punished by their courts.

ARTICLE VIII: MEASURES TO PREVENT AND INTERDICT TRAFFICKING IN WOMEN AND CHILDREN

1. The State Parties to the Convention shall provide sufficient means, training and assistance to their respective authorities to enable them to effectively conduct inquiries, investigations and prosecution of offences under this Convention.
2. The State Parties to the Convention shall sensitise their law enforcement agencies and the judiciary in respect of the offences under this Convention and other related factors that encourage trafficking in women and children.
3. The State Parties to the Convention shall establish a Regional Task Force consisting of officials of the Member States to facilitate implementation of the provisions of this Convention and to undertake periodic reviews.
4. The State Parties to the Convention may also, by mutual agreement, set up bilateral mechanisms to effectively implement the provisions of the Convention, including appropriate mechanisms for cooperation to interdict trafficking in women and children for prostitution.
5. The State Parties to the Convention shall exchange, on a regular basis, information in respect of agencies, institutions and individuals who are involved in trafficking in the region and also identify methods and routes used by the traffickers through land, water or air. The information so furnished shall include information of the offenders, their fingerprints, photographs, methods of operation, police records and records of conviction.
6. The State Parties to the Convention may consider taking necessary measures for the supervision of employment agencies in order to prevent trafficking in women and children under the guise of recruitment.
7. The State Parties to the Convention shall endeavour to focus preventive and development efforts on areas which are known to be source areas for trafficking.
8. The State Parties to the Convention shall promote awareness, inter-alia, through the use of the media, of the problem of trafficking in Women and Children and its underlying causes including the projection of negative images of women.

ARTICLE IX:
CARE, TREATMENT, REHABILITATION AND REPATRIATION OF THE VICTIMS

1. The State Parties to the Convention shall work out modalities for repatriation of the victims to the country of origin.
2. Pending the completion of arrangements for the repatriation of victims of cross-border trafficking, the State Parties to the Convention shall make suitable provisions for their care and maintenance. The provision of legal advice and health care facilities shall also be made available to such victims.
3. The State Parties to the Convention shall establish protective homes or shelters for rehabilitation of victims of trafficking. Suitable provisions shall also be made for granting legal advice, counselling, job training and health care facilities for the victims.
4. The State Parties to the Convention may also authorise the recognised non-governmental organisations to establish such protective homes or shelters for providing suitable care and maintenance for the victims of trafficking.
5. The State Parties to the Convention shall encourage recognised non-governmental organisations in efforts aimed at prevention, intervention and rehabilitation, including through the establishment of such protective homes or shelters for providing suitable care and maintenance for the victims of trafficking.

ARTICLE X:
IMPLEMENTATION

The State Parties to the Convention shall adopt, in accordance with their respective Constitutions, the legislative and other measures necessary to ensure the implementation of the Convention.

ARTICLE XI:
HIGHER MEASURES

The measures provided for in the Convention are without prejudice to higher measures of enforcement and protection accorded by relevant national laws and international agreements.

ARTICLE XII: SIGNATURE AND RATIFICATION

The Convention shall be open for signature by the Member States of SAARC at the Eleventh SAARC Summit at Kathmandu and thereafter, at the SAARC Secretariat at Kathmandu. It shall be subject to ratification. The instruments of Ratification shall be deposited with the Secretary General.

ARTICLE XIII: ENTRY INTO FORCE

This Convention shall enter into force on the fifteenth day following the day of the deposit of the seventh Instrument of Ratification with the Secretary General.

ARTICLE XIV: DEPOSITORY

The Secretary-General shall be the depository of this Convention and shall notify the Member States of signatures to this Convention and all deposits of Instruments of Ratification. The Secretary-General shall transmit certified copies of such instruments to each Member-State. The Secretary-General shall also inform Member States of the date on which this Convention will have entered into force in accordance with Article XIII.

IN WITNESS WHEREOF the undersigned, being duly authorised thereto by their respective Governments, have signed this Convention.

DONE at Kathmandu on this Fifth Day of January Two Thousand and Two, in nine originals, in the English Language, all texts being equally authentic.

M. MORSHED KHAN
Minister for Foreign Affairs
People's Republic of Bangladesh

JIGMI Y. THINLEY
Minister of Foreign Affairs
Kingdom of Bhutan

JASWANT SINGH
Minister of External Affairs
Republic of India

FATHULLA JAMEEL
Minister of Foreign Affairs
Republic of Maldives

RAM SHARAN MAHAT
Minister of Finance and Leader of the Delegation of Nepal
Kingdom of Nepal

ABDUL SATTAR
Minister of Foreign Affairs
Islamic Republic of Pakistan

TYRONNE FERNANDO
Minister of Foreign Affairs
Democratic Socialist Republic of Sri Lanka

References

Abraham, Margaret. 2000. *Speaking the Unspeakable: Marital Violence Among South Asians Immigrants in the United States*. Piscataway, NJ: Rutgers University Press.

Abu-Lughod, Lila. 2002. "Do Muslim Women Really Need Saving? Anthropological Reflections on Cultural Relativism and Its Others." *American Anthropologist* 104(3):783-90.

Adur, Shweta M. 2011. "Do Human Rights Endure Across Nation-State Boundaries? Analyzing the Experiences of Guest Workers." Pp.162-172 in *Human Rights in Our Own Backyard: Injustice and Resistance in the United States*, edited by W. T. Armaline, D. S. Glasberg, and B. Purkayastha. Philadelphia, PA: University of Pennsylvania Press.

Amin, Mohammad. 2010. *A Research Study on the Trends & Causes of Women Trafficking in NWFP, Pakistan*. Peshawar, Pakistan: Community Appraisal and Motivation Programme.

Anderson, Bridget and Julia O'Connell Davidson. 2003. *Is Trafficking in Human Beings Demand Driven? A Multi-Country Pilot Study*. Geneva, Switzerland: International Organization for Migration.

Appadurai, Arjun. 1990. *Modernity at Large*. Minneapolis, MN: University of Minnesota Press.

Appadurai, Arjun. 1993. "Number in the Colonial Imagination." Pp.314-40 in *Orientalism and the Postcolonial Predicament: Perspectives on South Asia*, edited by C. A. Breckenridge and P. van der Veer. Philadelphia, PA: University of Pennsylvania Press

Aradau, Claudia. 2008. *Rethinking Trafficking in Women: Politics out of Security*. New York: Palgrave Macmillan.

Armaline, William T., Davita S. Glasberg, and Bandana Purkayastha, eds. 2011. *Human Rights in Our Own Backyard: Injustice and Resistance in the United States*. Philadelphia, PA: University of Pennsylvania Press.

Aronowitz, Alexis A. 2001. "Smuggling and Trafficking in Human Beings: The Phenomenon, the Markets that Drive It and the Organisations that Promote It." *European Journal on Criminal Policy and Research* 9(2):163-95.

Aronowitz, Alexis A. 2002. "The United Nations Global Programme Against Trafficking in Human Beings: Research and Lessons Learned." *International Journal of Comparative and Applied Criminal Justice* 26(2):257-75.

Aronowitz, Alexis A. 2009. *Human Trafficking, Human Misery: The Global*

Trade in Human Beings. Westport, CT: Praeger.

Asian Development Bank. 2003. *Combating Trafficking of Women and Children in South Asia: Regional Synthesis Paper for Bangladesh, Nepal, and India*. Manila, Philippines: Asian Development Bank.

Awan, Zia A. and Nazish Brohi. 2000. *Shattered Dreams and Living Nightmares: Situational Analysis on Trafficking of Women and Children in Pakistan*. Islamabad, Pakistan: ActionAid.

Bales, Kevin. 2000. "Expendable People: Slavery in the Age of Globalization". *Journal of International Affairs* 53(2):461-84.

Bales, Kevin. 2004. *Disposable People: New Slavery in the Global Economy*. Berkley, CA: University of California Press.

Bales, Kevin. 2005. *Understanding Global Slavery: A Reader*. Berkley, CA: University of California Press.

Batstone, David. 2007. *Not for Sale: The Return of the Global Trade—and How We Can Fight It*. New York: HarperCollins.

Bernstein, Elizabeth. 2007. *Temporarily Yours: Intimacy, Authenticity, and the Commerce of Sex*. Chicago: The University of Chicago Press.

Bernstein, Elizabeth. 2010. "Militarized Humanitarianism Meets Carceral Feminism: The Politics of Sex, Rights, and Freedom in Contemporary Anti Trafficking Campaigns." *Signs* 36(1):45-71.

Bertone, Andrea M. 2000. "Sexual Trafficking in Women: International Political Economy and the Politics of Sex." *Gender Issues* 18(1):4-22.

Bile, K. M., J. A. R. H. Qureshi, S. A. H. Rizvi, S. A. A. Naqvi, A. Q. Usmani, and K. A. Lashari. 2010. "Human Organ and Tissue Transplantation in Pakistan: When a Regulation Makes a Difference." *Eastern Mediterranean Health Journal* 16(S):159-66.

Birkenthal, Sara. 2011. "Human Trafficking: A Human Rights Abuse with Global Dimensions." *Interdisciplinary Journal of Human Rights Law* 6(1): 27-40.

Brown, Louise. 2000. *Sex Slaves: The Trafficking of Women in Asia*. London, England: Virago.

Brysk, Alison. 2009. "Beyond Framing and Shaming: Human Trafficking, Human Security, and Human Rights." *Journal of Human Security* 5(3):8-21.

Brysk, Alison. 2012. "Rethinking Trafficking: Human Rights and Private Wrongs." Pp.73-87 in *From Human Trafficking to Human Rights: Reframing Contemporary Slavery*, edited by A. Brysk and A. Choi-Fitzpatrick. Philadelphia, PA: University of Pennsylvania Press.

Brysk, Alison and Austin Choi-Fitzpatrick, eds. 2012. *From Human Trafficking to Human Rights: Reframing Contemporary Slavery*. Philadelphia, PA: University of Pennsylvania Press.

Bukovska, Barbora. 2008. "Perpetrating Good: The Unlimited Consequences of International Human Rights Advocacy." *Sur-International*

Journal on Human Rights 5(9):7-20. Retrieved January 15, 2014 (http://www.surjournal.org/eng/conteudos/pdf/9/bukovska.pdf).

Bulbeck, Chilla. 1998. *Re-orienting Western Feminisms: Women's Diversity in a Postcolonial World*. Cambridge, England: Cambridge University Press.

Bush, Michael A. 2010. "Afghanistan and the Sex Trade." Pp.111-18 in *Sex Trafficking: A Global Perspective,* edited by K. A. McCabe and S. Manian. Lanham, MD: Lexington Books.

Cameron, Sally and Edward Newman, eds. 2008. *Trafficking in Human$: Social, Cultural and Political Dimensions*. Tokyo, Japan: United Nations University Press.

Chapkis, Wendy. 2003. "Trafficking, Migration, and the Law: Protecting Innocents, Punishing Immigrants." *Gender & Society* 17(6):923-37.

Chew, Dolores. 2006. "Gender, Migration and Trafficking: An Introduction." *Labour, Capital and Society* 39(2):1-18.

Chowdhury, Elora H. 2011. *Transnationalism Reversed: Women Organizing against Gendered Violence in Bangladesh*. Albany, NY: State University of New York.

Collins, Patricia H. 2009. *Black Feminist Thought: Knowledge, Consciousness, and the Politics of Empowerment*. 3rd ed. New York: Routledge.

Connell, R. W. 1985. "Theorizing Gender." *Sociology* 19(2):260-72.

Connell, R. W. 2005. "Change among the Gatekeepers: Men, Masculinities, and Gender Equality in the Global Arena." *Signs* 30(3):1801-25.

Crawford, Mary. 2010. *Sex Trafficking in South Asia: Telling Maya's Story*. London, England: Routledge.

Critelli, Filomena M. 2010. "Women's Rights=Human Rights: Pakistani Women against Gender Violence." *Journal of Sociology and Social Welfare* 37(2):135-60.

Dauer, Sheila. 2001. "Indivisible or Invisible: Women's Human Rights in the Public and Private Sphere." Pp.65-82 in *Women, Gender and Human Rights: A Global Perspective,* edited by M. Agosin. New Bruswick, NJ: Rutgers University Press.

Dickenson, Donna. 2006. "Philosophical Assumptions and Presumptions about Trafficking for Prostitution." Pp.43-53 in *Trafficking and Women's Rights,* edited by C. L. van den Anker and J. Doomenik. New York: Palgrave Macmillan.

Ditmore, Melissa. 2005. "Trafficking in Lives: How Ideology Shapes Policy." Pp.107-26 in *Trafficking and Prostitution Reconsidered: New Perspectives on Migration, Sex Work, and Human Rights,* edited by K. Kempadoo, J. Sanghera, and B. Pattanaik. Boulder, CO: Paradigm Press.

Doezema, Jo. 2002. "Who Gets to Choose? Coercion, Consent, and the UN Trafficking Protocol." *Gender and Development* 10(1):20-27.

Donnelly, Jack. 2007. "The Relative Universality of Human Rights." *Human Rights Quarterly* 29(2):281-306.

Ebbe, Obi N. I. 2008. "The Nature and Scope of Trafficking in Women and Children." Pp.17-32 in *Global Trafficking in Women and Children*, edited by O. N. I. Ebbe and D. K. Das. Boca Raton, FL: CRC Press.

Enterprise for Business & Development Management. 2009. "Baseline Study on Illegal Migration, Human Smuggling and Trafficking in Pakistan." Retrieved December 28, 2013 (http://www.befare.org/Baseline%20Survey.pdf).

Erturk, Yakun and Bandana Purkayastha. 2012. "Linking Research Policy and Action: A Look at the Work of the Special Rapporteur on Violence against Women." *Current Sociology* 60(2):142-60.

Espiritu, Yen L. 2007. *Asian American Women and Men: Love, Labour, Laws*. Lanham, MD: Rowman and Littlefield.

Farley, Melissa. 2003. *Prostitution, Trafficking, and Traumatic Stress*, ed. New York: The Haworth Maltreatment & Trauma Press.

Ferree, Myra M. 1990. "Beyond Separate Spheres." *Journal of Marriage and Family* 52(4): 866–87.

Finklea, Kristin M., Andrienne L. Fernandes-Alcantara, and Alison Siskin. 2011. "*Sex Trafficking of Children in the United States: Overview and Issues for Congress.*" Retrieved January 22, 2014 (https://www.fas.org/sgp/crs/misc/R41878.pdf).

Foner, Philip S. and Yuval Taylor. 1999. *Frederick Douglas: Selected Speeches and Writings*. Chicago: Lawrence Hill Books.

Fritz, Jan M., Sharon Doering, and F. B. Gumru. 2011. "Women, Peace, Security and the National Action Plans." *Journal of Applied Social Sciences* 5(1):1-23.

Gaer, Felice D. 2001. "Mainstreaming a Concern for the Human Rights of Women: Beyond Theory." Pp.98-124 in *Women, Gender and Human Rights: A Global Perspective*, edited by M. Agosin. New Bruswick, NJ: Rutgers University Press.

Gallagher, Anne T. 2010. *The International Law of Human Trafficking*. New York: Cambridge University Press.

Gibney, Mark and Sigrun Skogly. 2010. *Universal Human Rights and Extraterritorial Obligations*. Philadelphia, PA: University of Pennsylvania Press.

Gleditsch, Nils P., Peter Wallensteen, Mikael Eriksson, Margareta Sollenberg, and Havard Strand. 2002. "Armed Conflict, 1946-2001: A New Dataset." *Journal of Peace Research* 39(5): 615-37.

Glenn, Evelyn N. 2002. *Unequal Freedom: How Race and Gender Shaped American Citizenship and Labor*. Cambridge, MA: Harvard University Press.

Global Slavery Index. 2013. Nedlands, Australia: Walk Free Foundation.

Retrieved January 6, 2014 (http://www.globalslaveryindex.org/report/)

Goldman, Emma. 1910. *The White Slave Traffic*. New York: Mother Earth Publishing Association. Retrieved January 2, 2014 (http://theanarchistlibrary.org/library/Emma_Goldman_The_White_Slave_Traffic.html).

Gould A. 2001. *Developments in Swedish Social Policy: Resisting Dionysus*. London, England: Palgrave.

Grant, Melissa G. 2014. "The Price of a Sex Slave Rescue Fantasy." *New York Times*, May 30, p. A27.

Haerens, Margaret. 2012. *Human Trafficking: Global Viewpoints*. Farmington Hills, MI: Greenhaven Press.

Hahmi, Munaza. 2009. "Darul Aman in Punjab." *Dawn*, 23 August. Retrieved January 22, 2014 (http://archives.dawn.com/archives/54380).

Haider, Mahe N. 2005. *The Pakistan Thematic Group's Position Paper on Human Trafficking: Development of Conceptual Framework and Strategies to Combat Trafficking*. Islamabad, Pakistan: International Organization for Migration

Haque, Md. Shahidul. 2006. "Ambiguities and Confusions in Migration-Trafficking Nexus: A Development Challenge." Pp.3-20 in *Trafficking and the Global Sex Industry*, edited by K. Beeks and D. Amir. Lanham, MD: Lexington Books.

Holmes, Leslie. 2010. "Introduction: The Issue of Human Trafficking." Pp.1-17 in *Trafficking and Human Rights: European and Asia-Pacific Perspectives*, edited by L. Holmes. Cheltenham, England: Edward Elgar.

Hua, Julietta. 2011. *Trafficking Women's Human Rights*. Minneapolis, MN: University of Minnesota Press.

Hua, Julietta and Holly Nigorizawa. 2010. "US Sex Trafficking, Women's Human Rights, and the Politics of Representation." *International Feminist Journal of Politics* 12(3-4):401-23.

Huda, S. 2006. "Sex Trafficking in South Asia." *International Journal of Gynaecology & Obstetrics* 94(3):374-81.

Hukil, Roomana. 2013. *South Asia: Anti-Trafficking, Flesh Trade, and Human Rights*. Institute of Peace and Conflict Studies. Retrieved January 3, 2014 (http://www.ipcs.org/article/india/special-commentary-south-asia-anti-trafficking-flesh-trade-and-human-4116.html).

Hussein, Maliha and Shazreh Hussain. 2012. *Internal Trafficking of Women and Girls in Pakistan: A Research Study*. Islamabad, Pakistan: Aurat Foundation.

Icduygu, Ahmet and Sule Toktas. 2002. "How Do Smuggling and Trafficking Operate via Irregular Border Crossings in the Middle East? Evidence from Fieldwork in Turkey." *International Migration* 40(6):25-54.

International Labour Organization. 2013. *Report IV(1): Strengthening Action to End Forced Labour*. Geneva, Switzerland: International Labour Office.

International Labour Organization. 2014. *Profits and Poverty: The Economics of Forced Labour*. Geneva, Switzerland: International Labour Office.

Jalalzai, Musa Khan. 2002. *Women Trafficking and Prostitution in Pakistan and Afghanistan*. Lahore, Pakistan: Dua Publications.

Jeffreys, Elaine. 2003. "Transnational Prostitution—a Global Feminist Response?" *Australian Feminist Studies* 18(41):211-16.

Jeffreys, Sheila. 2009. *The Industrial Vagina: The Political Economy of the Global Sex Trade*. London, England: Routledge.

Jones, Tonisha R. 2010. "The Empirical Assessment of Human Trafficking in Washington State: Challenges, Roadblocks, and Barriers." PhD dissertation, Programme in Criminal Justice, Washington State University, Pullman.

Jordan, Ann. 2001. "Trafficking in Human Beings: The Slavery that Surrounds Us." *Global Issues* 6(2):15-18.

Jordan, Ann D. 2002. "Human Rights or Wrongs? The Struggle for a Right-based Response to Trafficking in Human Beings." pp. 28-37 in *Gender Trafficking and Slavery*, edited by R. Masika. Oxford, England: Oxfam.

Kara, Siddharth. 2011. "Supply and Demand: Human Trafficking in the Global Economy." *Harvard International Review* 33(2):66-77.

Kazim, Syed Faraz. 2008. "Organ Donation Law in Pakistan: An Overview of the Current Situation." *Journal of Pakistan Medical Association* 58(2):99-100.

Keegan, John. 1993. *A History of Warfare*. New York: Vintage Books.

Kempadoo, Kamala. 2005. "From Moral Panic to Global Justice: Changing Perspectives on Trafficking." Pp. vii-xxxiv in *Trafficking and Prostitution Reconsidered: New Perspectives on Migration, Sex Work, and Human Rights*, edited by K. Kempadoo, J. Sanghera, and B. Pattanaik. Boulder, CO: Paradigm Press.

Kertzer, David I. and Dominique Arel, eds. 2002. *Census and Identity. The Politics of Race, Ethnicity, and Language in National Censuses*. Cambridge, England: Cambridge University Press.

Konrad, Helga. 2008. "The Fight against Trafficking in Human Beings from the European Perspective." Pp.161-80 in *Trafficking in Human$: Social, Cultural and Political Dimension,* edited by S. Cameron and E. Newman. Tokyo, Japan: United Nations University Press.

Kostanyan, Arpine. 2012. "Human Rights and the Problem of Trafficking." pp. 17-25 in *Human Rights: Voices of the World's Young Activists*, edited by A. Omara-Otunnu, S. Mobilia and B. Purkayastha. London, England: Frontpage.

Kumar, Radha. 1990. *A History of Doing*. New Delhi: Zubaan Books.

Kyle, David and Rey Kolowski, eds. 2001. *Global Human Smuggling: Comparative Perspectives*. Baltimore, MD: The Johns Hopkins University Press.

Lawyers for Human Rights and Legal Aid. 1996. *Trafficking of Women and Children in Pakistan: The Flesh Trade Report 1995-1996*. Karachi, Pakistan: Lawyers for Human Rights and Legal Aid.

Lekorwe, M. and D. Mpabanga. 2007. "Managing Non-Governmental Organizations in Botswana." *The Innovation Journal* 12(3):1-18. Retrieved January 21, 2014 (http://www.innovation.cc/scholarly-style/lekorwe10final1draft.pdf).

Liempt, Ilse van. 2006. "Trafficking in Human Beings: Conceptual Dilemmas." Pp.27-42 in *Trafficking and Women's Rights*, edited by C. L. van den Anker and J. Doomenik. New York: Palgrave Macmillan.

Lobasz, Jennifer K. 2009. "Beyond Border Security: Feminist Approaches to Human Trafficking." *Security Studies* 18(2):319-44. doi: 10.1080/09636410902900020

Loff, Bebe and Jyoti Sanghera. 2004. "Distortions and Difficulties in Data for Trafficking." *Lancet* 363(9408):566. doi:10.1016/S0140-6736(04)15548-7

Masud Ali, A. K. M. 2005. "Treading along a Treacherous Trail: Research on Trafficking in Persons in South Asia." Pp. 141-64 in *Data and Research on Human Trafficking: A Global Survey*, edited by F. Laczko and E. Gozdziak. Geneva, Switzerland: International Organization for Migration.

McCabe, Kimberly A. and Sabita Manian, eds. 2010. *Sex Trafficking: A Global Perspective*. Lanham, MD: Lexington Books.

Merry, Sally E. 2006. *Human Rights and Gender Violence: Translating International Law into Local Justice*. Chicago: University of Chicago Press.

Mills, Bright. 2011. *Human Trafficking: Modern Day Slavery*. Bloomington, IN: Trafford Publishing.

Ministry of Home Affairs, Government of the People's Republic of Bangladesh. 2012. *Combating Human Trafficking: Bangladesh Country Report*.

Munir, Shafqat. 2003. "Trafficking, South Asia and Pakistan." *Himal South Asian* 16(9):40-42.

Musto, Jennifer L. 2010. "The NGO-ification of the Anti-trafficking Movement in the United States: A Case Study of the Coalition to Abolish Slavery and Trafficking." Pp.23-36 in *Sex Trafficking, Human Rights and Social Justice*, edited by T. Zheng. New York: Routledge.

Mutua, Makau. 2008 "Human Rights in Africa: The Limited Promise of Liberalism." *African Studies Review* 51(1):17-39.

Naples, Nancy. 2002. "Changing the Terms: Community Activism, Globalization, and the Dilemmas of Transnational Feminist Praxis." Pp.3-14 in *Women's Activism and Globalization: Linking Local Struggles and Transnational Politics*, edited by N. Naples and M. Desai. New York: Routledge.

Narayan, Anjana and Bandana Purkayastha. 2009. *Living Our Religions: Hindu and Muslim South Asian-American Women Narrate Their Experiences*. Stirling, VA: Kumarian Press.

Naqvi, Syed Ali A., Bux Ali, Farida Mazhar, Mirza N. Zafar, and Syed Abidul H. Rizvi. 2007. "A Socioeconomic Survey of Kidney Vendors in Pakistan." *Transplant International* 20(11):934-39.

Njiru, Roseanne and Bandana Purkayastha. Forthcoming. *Voices of Internally Displaced Persons in Kenya: A Human Rights Perspective*. London, England: Frontpage.

Nobles, Melissa. 2000. *Shades of Citizenship: Race and the Census in Modern Politics*. Stanford, CA: Stanford University Press.

Obokata, Tom. 2006. *Trafficking of Human Beings from a Human Rights Perspective: Towards a Holistic Approach*. Leiden, Netherlands: Koninklijke Brill NV.

Osiaty'nski, Wiktor. 2009. *Human Rights and their Limits*. New York: Cambridge University Press.

Othman, Zarina. 2006. "Human (In)security, Human Trafficking, and Security in Malaysia." Pp.47-60 in *Trafficking and the Global Sex Industry*, edited by K. Beeks and D. Amir. Lanham, MD: Lexington Books.

Outshoorn, Joyce. 2005. "The Political Debates on Prostitution and Trafficking of Women." *Social Politics* 12(1):141-55.

Pakistan Action Plan for Combating Human Trafficking. 2005. Islamabad, Pakistan: Ministry of Interior.

Pattanaik, Bandana. 2002. "Where Do We Go from Here?" Pp.217-30 in *Transnational Prostitution: Changing Patterns in a Global Context*, edited by S. Thorbek and B. Pattanaik. London, England: Zed Books.

Pearce, Tola O. 2011. "What Lies Beneath: Foundation of the U.S. Human Rights Perspective and Significance for Women." Pp.201-11 in *Human Rights in Our Own Backyard: Injustice and Resistance in the United States*, edited by W. T. Armaline, D. S. Glasberg, and B. Purkayastha. Philadelphia, PA: University of Pennsylvania Press.

Pearson, Elaine. 2004. *Coercion in the Kidney Trade? A Background Study on Trafficking in Human Organs Worldwide*. Eschborn, Germany: GTZ. Retrieved January 7, 2014 (http://www.childtrafficking.com/Docs/gtz_2004_organ_study_3 .pdf).

Purkayastha, Bandana. 2010. "Interrogating Intersectionality: Contemporary Globalization and Radicalized Gendering in the Lives of

Highly Educated South Asian Americans and their Children." *Journal of Intercultural Studies* 3(1):29-47.
Purkayastha, Bandana, Shweta M. Adur, Miho Iwata, Ranita Ray, and Trisha Tiamzon. 2012. *As the Leaves Turn Gold: Asian Americans and Experiences of Aging*. Lanham, MD: Rowman and Littlefield.
Purkayastha, Bandana and Shweta Majumdar. 2009. "Sex Trafficking in South Asia." Pp.185-202 in *Globalization and Third World Women*, edited by L. Lindio-McGovern and I. Wallimann. Farnham, England: Ashgate.
Purkayastha, Bandana and Kathryn S. Ratcliff. 2014. "Routine Violence: Intersectionality at the Interstices." Pp.19-43 in *Advances in Gender Research*. Vol. 18B, *Gendered Perspectives On Conflict And Violence*, edited by M. T. Segal and V. Demos. Bingley, England: Emerald Group Publishing Limited.
Ray, Ranita. 2011. "Sex Trafficking: In Our Backyard?" Pp.212-19 in *Human Rights in Our Own Backyard: Injustice and Resistance in the United States*, edited by W. T. Armaline, D. S. Glasberg, and B. Purkayastha. Philadelphia, PA: University of Pennsylvania Press.
Raymond, Janice G. 2002. "The New U.N. Trafficking Protocol." *Women's Studies International Forum* 25(5):503-14.
Rijken, Conny. 2003. *Trafficking in Persons: Prosecution from a European Perspective*. The Hague, Netherlands: T.M.C. Asser Press.
Rosenberg, Ruth. 2010. *Trafficking of Adult Men in the Europe and Eurasia Region*. United States Agency for International Development. Retrieved December 28, 2013 (http://lastradainternational.org/lsidocs/Trafficking%20of%20Men%20Draft_final.pdf).
Saeed, Fouzia. 2002. *Taboo: The Hidden Culture of a Red Light Area*. Karachi, Pakistan: Oxford University Press.
Salt, John. 2000. "Trafficking and Human Smuggling: A European Perspective." *International Migration* 38(3):31-56.
Sanghera, Jyoti. 2005. "Unpacking the Trafficking Discourse." Pp.3-24 in *Trafficking and Prostitution Reconsidered: New Perspectives on Migration, Sex Work, and Human Rights*, edited by K. Kempadoo, J. Sanghera, and B. Pattanaik. Boulder, CO: Paradigm Press.
Sarwar, Beena. 1997. "Rights-South Asia: White Slavery Still a Thriving Trade." Retrieved Dec 18, 2013 (http://www.ipsnews.net/1997/12/rights-south-asia-white-slavery-still-a-thriving-trade/).
Schauer, Edward J. and Elizabeth M. Wheaton. 2006. "Sex Trafficking into the United States: A Literature Review." *Criminal Justice Review* 31(2):146-69.
Segrave, Marie, Sanja Milivojevic, and Sharon Pickering. 2009. *Sex Trafficking: International Context and Response*. Portland, OR: Willian Publishing.

Sen, Amartya. 1998. "Universal Truths: Human Rights and the Westernizing Illusion," *Harvard International Review* 20(3):40-43.

Sen, Sankar and P. M. Nair. 2005. *Trafficking in Women and Children in India*. Hyderabad, India: Orient Longman.

Seshu, Meena and Nandinee Bandhopadhyay. 2009. "How the Development Industry Imagines Sex Work." *Development* 52(1):13-17. doi:10.1057/dev.2008.86

Shah, Raffique. 2004. "From Foreign-used Cars to Foreign-used Kidneys." Retrieved December 13, 2013 (http://trinicenter.com/Raffique/2004/Aug/).

Shelley, Louise. 2010. *Human Trafficking: A Global Perspective*. New York: Cambridge University Press.

Shimazono, Yosuke. 2007. "The State of the International Organ Trade: A Provisional Picture Based on Integration of Available Information." *Bulletin* 85(12):955-62. Retrieved January 30, 2014 (http://www.who.int/bulletin/volumes/85/12/06-039370/en/).

Sietske, Altink. 1995. *Stolen Lives: Trading Women into Sex and Slavery*. London, England: Scarlet Press.

Sinha, Indrani and Shamita D. Dasgupta. 2009. *Mothers for Sale: Women in Kolkata's Sex Trade*. Kolkata, India: Dasgupta-Alliance.

Skeldon, Ronald. 2000. "Trafficking: A Perspective from Asia." *International Migration* 38(3):7-30. doi: 10.1111/1468-2435.00113

Sleightholme, Carolyn and Indrani Sinha. 1996. *Guilty without Trial: Women in Sex Trade in Calcutta*. Kolkata, India: Stree.

Sulaimanova, Sultanat. 2006. "Trafficking in Women from the Former Soviet Union for the Purpose of Sexual Exploitation." Pp.61-75 in *Trafficking and the Global Sex Industry*, edited by K. Beeks and D. Amir. Lanham, MD: Lexington Books.

Thorbek, Susanne. 2002. "Prostitution in a Global Context: Changing Patterns." Pp.1-10 in *Transnational Prostitution: Changing Patterns in a Global Context*, edited by S. Thorbek and B. Pattanaik. London, England: Zed Books.

Tripp, Aili M., Myra M. Ferree, and Christina Ewing, eds. 2013. *Gender, Violence, and Human Security: Critical Feminist Perspectives*. New York: New York University Press.

United Nations Development Programme. 2003. *From Challenges to Opportunities: Responses to Trafficking and HIV/AIDS in South Asia*. Retrieved December 18, 2013 (https://www.unodc.org/documents/hivaids/publications/FromChallengestoOpportunities.pdf).

United Nations Development Programme. 2007. *Human Trafficking and HIV: Exploring Vulnerabilities and Responses in South Asia*. Colombo, Sri Lanka: UNDP Regional Centre. Retrieved January 10, 2014 (http://www.unodc.org/documents/hiv-aids/publications/human_traffick_hiv_undp2007.pdf).

United Nations Educational, Scientific, and Cultural Organization. (Nd) *Trafficking and HIV/AIDS Project*. Retrieved January 25, 2014 (http://www.unescobkk.org/culture/diversity/trafficking-hiv/projects/trafficking-%20statistics-%20project/updated-data-comparison/).

United Nations Educational, Scientific, and Cultural Organization. (Nd). *Trafficking Statistics Project*. Retrieved January 7, 2014 (http://www.unescobkk.org/culture/diversity/trafficking-hiv/projects/trafficking-statistics-project/).

United Nations High Commissioner for Human Rights. 2002. *Recommended Principles and Guidelines on Human Rights and Human Trafficking*. Retrieved January 7, 2014 (http://www.ohchr.org/Documents/Publications/Traffickingen.pdf).

United Nations High Commissioner for Refugees. 2014. UNHCR Country Operations Profile–Pakistan. Retrieved January 7, 2014 (http://www.unhcr.org/pages/49e487016.html).

United Nations Office on Drugs and Crime. 2006. *Trafficking in Persons: Global Patterns*. Retrieved January 15, 2014 (http://www.unodc.org/pdf/traffickinginpersons_report_2006-04.pdf).

United Nations Office on Drugs and Crime. 2007. *Responding to Trafficking for Sexual Exploitation in South Asia*. New York: United Nations. Retrieved January 6, 2014 (http://www.ungift.org/docs/ungift/pdf/world/INDIA.pdf).

United Nations Office on Drugs and Crime. 2008. *Human Trafficking: An Overview*. New York: United Nations. Retrieved December 28, 2013 (http://www.ungift.org/docs/ungift/pdf/knowledge/ebook.pdf).

United States Department of State. 2006. *Fact Sheet: Distinctions between Human Smuggling and Human Trafficking*. Retrieved December 4, 2012 (www.state.gov/m/ds/hstcenter/90434.htm).

United States Department of State. 2012. *Trafficking in Persons Report*. Retrieved December 18, 2013 (http://www.state.gov/j/tip/rls/tiprpt/2012/192351.htm).

United States Department of State. 2013. *Trafficking in Persons Report*. Retrieved January 8, 2014 (http://www.state.gov/j/tip/rls/tiprpt/2013/).

Veen, Marjolein van der. 2001. "Rethinking Commodification and Prostitution: An Effort at Peacemaking in the Battles over Prostitution." *Rethinking Marxism* 13(2):30-51.

Watkin, Kenneth. 2004. "Controlling the Use of Force: A Role for Human Rights Norms in Contemporary Armed Conflict." *The American Journal of International Law* 98(1):1-34.

Wilson, Annie. 2012. "Notes From the Field: Trafficking Risks for Refugees." *Societies Without Borders* 7(1):100-118.

Yousaf, Faisal. 2006. "Civil Society Response to Human Trafficking in South Asia," *Forced Migration Review*, 25 May, p.16. Retrieved January 30, 2014 (http://www.fmreview.org/FMRpdfs/FMR25/FMR25full.pdf).

Zakar, Muhammad Z. 2004. *Aids, Culture and Body Politics in Pakistan*. Lage, Germany: Jacobs.

Zhang, Sheldon X. 2007. *Smuggling and Trafficking in Human Beings: All Roads Lead to America*. West Port, CT: Praeger.

Zheng, Tiantian. 2010. *Sex Trafficking, Human Rights and Social Justice*. New York: Routledge.

